F O G
the

Lifted

A Clinician's Victorious Journey with ADHD

Kristin Seymour, MSN, RN, AHCNS-BC

For consultation, speaking engagements or professional meeting requests, please send inquiries to ksfoglifted@gmail.com or visit ADHDfoglifted.com

Cover and Internal Design by Kim Torbeck, Imbue Design imbuedsign@fuse.net

Printed in the United States of America

Library of Congress Cataloging-in-Publication Data
Seymour, Kristin-author.
The Fog Lifted: A Clinician's Victorious Journey with ADHD.

ISBN 978-0-692-68656-0

Physician Endorsement

Kristin's story is nothing short of staggering. Knowing Kristin as an extraordinary nurse, physician liaison, and outreach leader, I never knew what came before. She was simply a high energy, high caliber professional whose impact was far reaching and significant. I always told her, "Whatever they pay you... it's not enough." I had no idea of the struggles she faced and conquered. Learning her story and challenges I was deeply moved by her hard work, determination, persistence and ambition. She turned "thinking differently" into her biggest asset. By learning to harness her energy instead of letting it pull her in different directions, she has been able to function successfully as a high caliber professional. Her story informs me in several aspects of parenting. The descriptions of struggle are generous and the victories leave one feeling hopeful. Kristin's energy and positivity are contagious on the page and in her every endeavor. She is an inspiration for those who do not believe that their dreams are attainable.
— *Scott C. Silvestry, MD, Thoracic and Cardiovascular Surgery, Florida Hospital Transplant Institute*

Endorsements

Brave, poignant, and true, Kristin Seymour's dramatic story of pain and defeat followed by joy and triumph and now a career of giving back makes for a compelling call to the world to recognize the courage, grit, and talent this woman — and millions of others with ADHD truly have. An inspiration. Bravo!
— *Edward (Ned) M. Hallowell, MD, ADHD Expert and Bestselling Author, Boston, Massachusetts*

The Fog Lifted is a testament to what can be accomplished when patients and physicians work together in partnership. Seymour's success is a result of her determination, a committed family, and medical professionals who were willing to listen and take the time to truly understand her condition. In a time where the answer to many disorders is a prescription, The Fog Lifted reminds us all that treatment is a multidisciplinary effort. I believe this story brings hope to many who are facing similar challenges in their own lives.
— *Nikoleta S. Kolovos, MD, Washington University School of Medicine, St. Louis Children's Hospital*

I truly admire and appreciate the honesty portrayed in this book. It means so much for all who struggle with ADD or ADHD to hear about the journey from the perspective of someone who also functions in a clinical role. This book provides optimism, which is so important when adequate mental health support continues to be such an issue in society.

— *Stephanie Hess, MD, Boulder Community Health,*
Senior Clinical Instructor, University of Colorado Health

The Fog Lifted is a must read for educators who work with students with ADD or ADHD. Seymour's book provides an honest portrayal of the internal struggles and demands of living with these conditions. When parents, teachers and the medical community work together as a team, they can provide the student with an invaluable learning program. Seymour is a testament as to how one can overcome obstacles and achieve their lifelong dreams.

— *Laura K. Bartels, M.Ed., ESL Teacher, K-8,*
Thomasboro Academy, Charlotte, North Carolina

Acknowledgements

I would like to express my gratitude to the people who have walked — and continue to walk — with me on my journey:

Thank you to my amazing friends who provided support in publishing this book — those who talked things over, read, wrote, offered comments, and allowed me to quote their remarks — I am most grateful.

I would like to thank Kim Torbeck for enabling me to bring my manuscript to life. Your patience, constant support, and honest feedback, in addition to your graphic design and professional contributions, truly made this publication a reality.

Thank you to Patti Crimmins-Reda for being my mentor, supervisor, and friend. You always believed in me and my passion for nursing. I am confident that I would NOT be where I am today professionally without your advice, support and guidance.

Dr. Garrett C. Burris, you are a lifesaver. Words cannot express my sincere gratitude for all you've done. You were a life line for me when times were tough. You are a brilliant clinician, and a caring man with an impeccable bedside manner. You are truly devoted to your patients.

I am forever appreciative of my family — my parents and my siblings, Scott, Karen and John Paul. You all loved me at my best and worst and NEVER gave up on me even when I was close to giving up on myself. I am grateful for your forgiveness when I hurt you with my impulsive outbursts and occasional mean behavior. Thanks for tolerating my unusual and sometimes bizarre idiosyncrasies.

I dedicate this book to my beacon,

my lighthouse, my compass,

my best friend,

my greatest cheerleader,

my amazing husband, Jim —

the love of my life.

Without your patience, kindness,

unconditional love, and support,

I would not have my "happily ever after!"

You and our beautiful daughters

are my greatest treasures.

Contents

"I attribute my success to this: I never gave or took any excuse."

— Florence Nightingale

1

Treading Water

Have you ever been treading water... deep water, far from land?

If so, then you know how hard it is to kick and paddle furiously to keep your head above water, all while trying to conserve energy so you can make it to shore without drowning. You know how important, and seemingly impossible, it is to keep breathing and not panic, to stay focused on the swim ahead.

If you know how it feels to tread water like this, then you know how I've felt for most of my life.

I have ADHD. Like the frantic swimmer, I know what it's like to fight and fight and seem to go nowhere. I know what it's like to kick your hardest only to sink below the surface and feel like you're drowning.

I had a tutor in **every** subject during high school and know the effect ADHD can have on self-esteem.

I know unconditional love from my family who supported me through the worst times.

I have struggled, failed, and been disappointed. I know what it feels like to be distracted, unproductive, careless, and impulsive.

I also know what it's like to, through trial and effort, finally find your footing and propel yourself a little closer to land. I know what it feels like when the waves around you calm and you can finally see the shore in sight.

This book is about my journey living with ADHD. I hope that in sharing my story, I will help others who are struggling, and provide insight for the parents, teachers, friends, family, and therapists of anyone who is living with ADHD.

Recognizing and treating underlying ADHD, which negatively affected me for years, was a pivotal turning point.

"When you know your why, you can endure any how," (*Victor Frankl, quoted from* <u>On Fire</u>,

by John O'Leary, 2016). Once I knew my why,
I figured out how.

I was scattered, unable to focus and frustrated.
However, I was able to implement the recommendations from the multidisciplinary team and swim
to success.

I am confident that underlying ADHD enables
me to be positive, productive, have the ability
to think on my feet, and multi-task. These
combined qualities have resulted in personal and
professional success. (I often have Plan B ready
before Plan A blows up.)

"If you take responsibility for yourself you will
develop a hunger to accomplish your dreams."
(*Les Brown*).

What an honest and true statement! The
human mind is an amazing gift that many do
not utilize to its full potential. With awareness,
accountability, willpower, focus, and inner
strength, you can achieve anything. It is up to
you to be what you desire to be. I was NOT going
to quit. I was going to be a nurse someday.

Following years of struggles, recognizing
ADHD at age 19, seeking high caliber physicians,
and committing myself to a rigorous program,
I found true self-love. I am a happily married

woman of 19 years to an amazing man, the mother of two incredible daughters, and an Advanced Practice Nurse at a nationally renowned medical center.

I have achieved my goals, both professionally and personally. By sharing my own experiences, as well as the expertise of doctors and therapists who specialize in ADHD, I hope to help others with ADHD manage their condition. By offering advice on learning programs, parenting techniques, and self-regulation, I hope to help those living with ADHD discover the passions and talents that make them unique.

The most important lessons learned during my journey are to have faith and never quit.

I worked hard, never gave up, faced challenges and was victorious. I know what it feels like to have ADHD, and to be happy, focused, peaceful, and most importantly, have true self-love.

Breathe, focus, and swim... you can do it!

"Life is not measured by the number of breaths we take, but by the moments that take our breath away."

— MAYA ANGELOU

2

ADHD to the Rescue

This is a true story.*

March 17, 2016 (0710 AM)

I was on a plane heading to Naples, Florida for a quick weekend visit with my parents — sans kids and husband. I was ready to chill and visit my parents for a few days.

As the plane pulled away from the gate and headed for the runway, it suddenly stopped, turned around, and started back toward the terminal. The flight attendant keyed the intercom.

"Ladies and Gentleman, we need you to remain seated, we are returning to the gate." My heart stopped; Oh no! Something is not right! Semi-seriously, I said to the girl sitting next to me, "I hope it isn't terrorists."

"Me too," she replied, and we nervously

looked up toward the front of the plane for any indication of what was happening. The attendants had not stated the reason for our return, so we were all in the dark.

I was seated in row 22. I looked up and saw a man in row 6, probably in his late 50's or early 60's, stand up. His shirt was drenched — completely soaked through. I said to the girl sitting next to me, "I think that man is having a heart attack."

"How would you know that?" she asked.

"Three things: first, the time of day. Most heart attacks occur in the morning due to circadian rhythm; research shows this to be true. Second, his age. And third, the way he is so diaphoretic (sweaty)."

Without hesitation, I identified myself as an Advanced Practice Nurse to the flight attendant standing next to my row, and let her know that I would be able to assist if needed. The flight attendant said they were ok, but would let me know if that changed.

Two minutes later, I heard an announcement: "Lady in the back of the plane, with the white jeans, the nurse, we need you at the front of the plane ... NOW!"

Instinctively, I unbuckled my seat belt, ran to the front of the aisle, and deplaned with the attendant who was waiting for me. As I walked through the threshold, I saw the man from row 6. His skin was grey, he was dripping with sweat, and he looked terrified. I verified with the flight attendants that 911 and the EMS had been called, and that the AED was nearby (it was on floor next to me).

At this point, the patient, his wife, two flight attendants, and I were ten feet from the plane on the jet bridge walkway. His wife was crying and scared; the patient was short of breath, looked to be in distress, and was sitting in a wheelchair.

I took his hand, squatted down next to him, and calmly explained my role as I began to assess him.

I checked his pulse and found his heart rate to be 52 and regular. He informed me that he had a heart attack a month ago, and had a stent inserted (an appliance to keep vessels open). I asked him if he took his aspirin that morning — he did. I administered another aspirin. I knew how important it is to keep blood thin, especially with a stent placed weeks ago; we didn't want a clot to form.

The incidence of a second heart attack is

not uncommon within 30 days of an initial heart attack. The possibility of a near fatal heart rhythm could have been another cause.

At that point I had no way of knowing exactly what was happening to this man, but I was 90% sure he was having some kind of cardiac event. Based on that, I administered oxygen via face-mask to increase oxygen to his heart.

Keep in mind, this was all occurring in a non-clinical environment, with no blood pressure cuff, no ECG machine, no telemetry; nothing but an AED to use if he became pulseless, and a medication box that no one could use but a licensed medical professional. In fact, the attendants could not administer the oxygen as it is considered a medication. Many people are unaware that aspirin and oxygen are medications, and that not just anyone can administer medications to a patient.

The patient started to "feel better" after about five minutes. EMTs arrived about ten minutes later. I gave them a report, and gave my card with my cell phone number on it to the patient's wife. I then turned to the patient to try to reassure him.

I will never forget him looking in my eyes and asking me, "Am I going to be okay?" Having no idea if he would, with 100% certainty, I held his hand and replied, "You are going to be fine, we are doing everything in our power to help you be okay. You stay strong."

I instructed the EMTs to take the patient to Barnes-Jewish Hospital (BJH) where I work, as it is a Level One Center and this was a complex case since he had a heart attack just four weeks ago. The nearest hospital (only a five mile difference) may not have the advanced therapies necessary to treat complex heart disease or cardiogenic shock. The EMTs placed him on the gurney and off they went.

(0736 AM)

I got back on the plane, and called my boss, Patti, who is the Executive Patient Care Director of the Heart and Vascular Program at BJH. I informed her of the events that had just occurred and that the patient was en route.

She made sure that I was ok (she is amazing!), then said she would meet the patient in the cath lab and take great care of him. Patti said she would text me an update when we landed.

Back on the plane the patients' brothers and sister-in-law were crying and scared. I reassured them, but I literally prayed for the rest of the flight that he would live.

(0836 AM)
The patient was at the BJH cath lab being worked on. He had no further damage to his heart, but as I suspected, he was having a cardiac event that was very serious and potentially fatal.

March 19, 2016
The patient was cared for and did amazingly well. He was discharged and sent home with a heart monitor. This story could have had a much different outcome had we been in the air a few minutes earlier on March 17.

His wife called me in tears on Sunday, March 20. She thanked me for facilitating everything and helping them. She called me her "angel," and was so appreciative that they would be able to celebrate her husband's birthday together in just three days.

March 23, 2016
I sent the patient's wife a "Happy Birthday" text message for her husband's 60th birthday, and this was her text response: *"Thank you so much Kristin!*

Things are really working out thanks to you! We owe you everything!"

It was an amazing feeling to be able to focus and make critical decisions, to have a clear mind, and to be able to help this patient.

I was able to remember my training and everything I had learned in my career. I was able to remain calm and focused, without medication, and successfully help a patient in a highly chaotic and stressful situation. I know the adrenaline, my training, and even my ADHD(!), enabled me to help him — and resulted in a positive outcome.

Rather than sitting back and not getting involved (as so many people seem to do these days), I impulsively gave my unsolicited offer to help to the flight attendant in my aisle. Then, when urgently called to the front of the plane, I did not hesitate or allow fear to stop me from rushing up there to do the right thing. Finally, when thrown into this emergency situation in a jet bridge with everyone looking to me to solve the problem, I was able to hyperfocus and deliver.

How ironic that something that was once my biggest detriment, now had become an asset, helping me react without fear or hesitation, and possibly helping me to save a life!

I received an extremely heartfelt letter of thanks from the patient's wife on March 29. When I opened the envelope, I found a handwritten note that said: *"God sent you when we needed help the most. To all the people who don't believe in angels?! They never met you! Thank you Kristin."* The letter is reprinted with permission below:

March 24, 2016

Dear Kristin,

There are just not enough words to express the gratitude we feel for everything you did to help us on the morning of March 17. When my husband had all the symptoms of a heart attack as we were backing away from the gate on our flight to Florida that morning, it was almost as if God, Himself, sent you.

You appeared as if out of nowhere and did everything you could not only to help Bill, but reassure me that everything was going to be ok. You called ahead to the hospital, let them know the little you knew of his background, gave them your assessment, notified your boss what happened... basically took care of everything for me. All I had to do was get to Barnes with him and let the doctors there take over.

Patti came to me in the waiting room and introduced herself, and told me that you contacted her. She then did everything she could to make the whole ordeal as easy for me as possible. She told me they would work with the insurance company, and holy cow... that was HUGE! (I had gotten nothing but the runaround from the insurance people — to have an advocate like that on your side is humbling).

EVERYONE at Barnes has been wonderful, and beyond helpful. As weird as it seems, I cannot imagine being SO lucky... for my husband to be this ill, but to be surrounded by absolute angels in our time of need.

I just want to thank you — from the bottom of my heart. Bill and I are expecting to meet our first grandchild on October 27 of this year. Our daughter is engaged to be married in August 2017. Because of you and all the wonderful people at Barnes, I am confident that he will be here for these special moments in life. Our son and his wife, along with our daughter and her fiancé, wanted me to let you know how incredibly grateful they are as well. Their dad means the world to them.

You were the first link in the chain that saved my husband's life. Know that you will be in our prayers of gratitude for the rest of our lives.

God Bless and keep you!
Marla and Bill

Following the cardiac catheterization on March 17 which revealed multiple blockages to various arteries, the physicians agreed to monitor the patient's heart and test his cardiac function. Doing further intervention could have been risky without additional information as he had just had a stent placed four weeks before. The diffuse eccentric plaque found March 17 led the physicians to request to present his cardiac interventional case live at the 2016 American College of Cardiology National Conference in Chicago.

April 3, 2016
The Washington University interventionalists at Barnes Jewish Hospital performed a live cardiac intervention and stent placement on the patient that was shared via video stream/satellite with thousands of cardiologists at the conference. The procedure was shared in an effort to collaborate with the best, as well as teach — for the greater good — how to treat this complex cardiac condition. The patient did beautifully and tolerated the procedure well.

As I reflect on this incredible outcome, a number of "what if's?" come to mind.

What if I didn't plan a last minute trip to see my parents? What if the plane had taken off just a few minutes earlier? What if I didn't speak up to the flight attendant? What if the patient hadn't been taken to Barnes-Jewish Hospital to receive treatment by some of the highest caliber cardiologists in the country? What if his case wasn't so complex that it merited a live presentation before thousands of the world's top cardiologists at the largest national Cardiology conference?

What if I didn't have ADHD?

Would I have reacted the same? Would I have hesitated, or shied away? I'd like to think that I still would have done the right thing, but I believe that this was a prime example of how ADHD has had a positive effect on my life.

My ability to be hyperfocused** in this situation and help the patient at a critical moment was the result of my ADHD.

This may seem like a bold statement. Indeed, I would never have even considered that my ADHD could prove to be such an asset... when the fog still surrounded me.

---

* In regard to patient confidentiality and privacy laws, I have been given full permission by the parties involved to share this true story.
** Being hyperfocused makes a person with ADHD so intensely focused on a task that they may not even notice the world around them.

"You miss 100% of the shots you don't take."

— Wayne Gretzky

3

There Is No I in TEAM

"A Nurse." This was my response to the question, "What do you want to be when you grow up?"

For as long as I can remember, I wanted to be a nurse.

Every doll, figurine, stuffed animal, and Christmas ornament I ever owned became a nurse in my hands — complete with the nurse's dress, white cap, and stethoscope. The toys and tokens didn't always come with a cap, little stethoscope, or first aid kit. However, my mom would take me to a store called Aunt Heidi's Corner in Westport. There, I could find all the specific accessories and accents necessary to outfit my dolls, animals, and ornaments as nurses to my satisfaction. I would save my allowance to buy the items. My mother drove me and once we returned home, we dressed them up together.

There was never a doubt in my mind that I was going to be a nurse because I always loved taking care of others. I vividly remember riding my bike to my grandparents' house as a child and feeling such joy taking care of them. One specific instance was after my grandmother had surgery and returned home from the hospital, I visited her every day as I was fortunate to live only a short bike ride away. I remember bringing her 7-Up and crackers and massaging her feet with lotion to help her feel better. And whether it was applying a simple bandage to my baby brother's skinned knee or bringing crackers to my grandmother, I was ready and willing to take care of anyone, anytime.

As I peddled away, my grandmother would call out to me, "Thanks, Florence … we couldn't have done it without you!" I loved when she called me Florence because Florence Nightingale was my hero. My grandmother believed in me and believed that I would be a wonderful nurse someday.

When I had my tonsils removed in 1981, my parents brought me to Queeny Tower Restaurant for ice cream after the surgery. I remember sitting there at the table thinking, I am going to be a nurse someday and I am going to work at this hospital. Back then, it was called Barnes Hospital and it was, and still is, a massive medical center, filled with people working to help others. This was my dream.

Sadly, I worried that I would never achieve this dream because I absolutely **hated** school. I had a keen awareness of my real abilities early on, and the fact that I **REALLY** wanted to do well in school. Yet, my trouble with focus sabotaged my best efforts.

I was a full-term, nine-pound, healthy baby. Everyone said I was calm and peaceful. My mom says I rarely cried as a baby and slept through the night when I was only two months old. I grew up in suburban St. Louis with happily married parents and three siblings — an older brother, Scott, a younger sister, Karen (two years younger to the day!), and a younger brother, John Paul.

We played outside every day after school, either climbing trees, sledding, or riding bikes. We were encouraged to be active outside and not exist as "couch potatoes." This was the early 80s, so *iPads* and *iPods* wouldn't exist for another twenty years, and *Atari* was the only option as far as gaming was concerned. Since ready-made entertainment wasn't always available, kids played outside and actually used their imagination to make up games.

We were allowed 30 minutes of TV per night, including weekends, and only after sunset. Examples of the situational comedies we were allowed to watch were *Charles in Charge, Family Ties, The Golden Girls,* and *Empty Nest.* We were pretty sheltered. For example, we weren't allowed to watch *Tom and Jerry, The A Team,* or *The Dukes of Hazzard,* as our parents considered those shows too violent.

Phone calls were also restricted to 30 minutes per night. My parents considered watching television and talking on the phone "privileges," and if we acted up or didn't complete our homework assignments, they would take them away from us without question.

Some might consider these restrictions controlling; however, they were effective, forcing us to complete chores and homework, and encouraging active play outside.

Recess and physical education were part of daily curriculum at our schools as well as at home. Our parents, pediatrician, and teachers strongly believed that all kids, especially those who found it difficult to sit still, should have a physical outlet during the school day.

My brother, Scott, was a gifted athlete. He would pick up a tennis racquet for the first time, and within weeks play like John McEnroe. Or he might find a soccer ball, and within days play like Pelé. It was amazing. He was also a decent student. Scott was, and still is, hilarious. If anyone can make you laugh or find the humor in something, it is Scott.

My sister, Karen, was really good at sports, well-liked by her peers, and successful academically. She graduated at the top of her class in high school, and was on student council during most of her academic career.

My younger brother, John Paul, who is ten years younger than me, was adored by the entire family. He was the baby and could do no wrong.

I, on the other hand, was neither a scholar nor a gifted athlete. However, I was a compassionate person who loved everyone, especially when it came to cheering people up or caring for them when they were sick. My mom has always said, "Kristin can make friends with people in the movie theatre line," or, "Kristin has NEVER met a stranger."

My parents frequently reminded me that my genuine love and compassion were my "gifts."

I suppose that even though my parents constantly reminded me of my gift of love and compassion for others, I probably felt somewhat subpar or ashamed about not being a good athlete or scholar. I also probably felt a little inferior that I was never on student council or participated on many committees, unlike my siblings. Of course, we had NO idea what ADHD was, and that I had it back then. We had no idea why, as hard as I tried, success was halted by my impulsivity and inability to focus. When I was growing up, my parents and teachers probably thought that it was just my unique personality, and that I would "outgrow" some of the ADHD traits, but that never happened.

Overall, my social life was good and fairly typical. I didn't have issues with making friends, keeping friends, or getting into trouble.

I loved doing art projects, ballet, and tap dancing as a child. These activities brought me happiness, a creative outlet, and helped to ease my anxiety. One of my favorite parts about dance class was wearing the same leotard and tights as everyone else. I loved that we all looked the same and no one knew if we were "smart" or not. While dancing, we were moving around, which eliminated any pressure to sit still and focus. Looking like the other girls made me *feel* like the other girls. Meaning, maybe no one would notice that my brain was foggy and in three different places while we were sitting there listening to the instructor before dancing.

As difficult as it is to plan for and maintain extracurricular activities due to schedule conflicts, carpool, and work, the positive outcome of such activities is *essential* for an ADHD child's confidence and academic success.

Renowned parenting and ADHD expert Dr. Edward M. Hallowell describes the love that children with ADHD have for activities in which they are successful, and describes them as a vital component toward building their self-confidence and self-image. According to Hallowell, "Due to repeated failures, misunderstandings, mislabelings, and all manner of other emotional mishaps, children with ADD usually develop problems with their self-image and self-esteem."

Therefore, children with ADHD are happy and

thrive when participating in activities in which they excel. They gain confidence and increased self-esteem by being successful. These activities must be supported and encouraged by parents.

When children excel at something, they strive to achieve greatness, while also developing confidence and, ultimately, "self-love." When a child experiences "self-love" as well as increased confidence, they are more secure when facing life's difficult challenges, such as peer pressure and schoolwork.

Looking back on my childhood, I realize that I experienced "self-love" when I attended art classes or performed dance routines. I thrived doing these activities and felt happy. So, naturally, I was more confident and felt good about myself.

According to Deborah Khoshaba, PsyD, "self-love is a state of appreciation for oneself that grows from actions that support our physical, psychological, and spiritual growth. Self-love is dynamic; it grows by actions that mature us. When we act in ways that expand self-love in us, we begin to accept much better our weaknesses as well as our strengths, have less need to explain away our short-comings, have compassion for ourselves as human beings struggling to find personal meaning, are more centered in our life purpose and values, and expect living fulfillment through our own efforts."

I was fortunate during my journey of self-love because — whether it was driving me to practice, watching me perform, cheering me on at a game, celebrating a victory, or consoling a loss — my parents were always present and there for me.

My parents encouraged all of us to do what we excelled at, but this was even more important in my case because of my struggles with attention, impulsivity, and focus.

The only stipulation was that we were not allowed to quit anything ... ever.

We were encouraged to try everything in which we showed interest, whether it was sports, musical instruments, dance, art, gymnastics, whatever ... as long as we finished what we started.

In their eyes, trying and failing was better than never trying something we were interested in, or worse, quitting something we started before completion.

In the fourth grade, I desperately wanted to quit the soccer team. I was so sick of going to practice and having the coach never play me in games. It was frustrating to attend practice, try my best, but never play. I have to admit, I was not very fast or very good at soccer, but I always tried my best. But, despite my protests, my parents refused to let me quit mid-season. They said, "There are no quitters in this family, and you'll finish the season."

I wasn't happy about it, but I finished the season. I didn't go on to become a great soccer player that season. In fact, once the season was over, I resigned myself from soccer for good. But, instead of moping, I became the best bench-warmer and cheerleader for my teammates. I may not have been a star on the field, but I had a purpose on that team, and I was able to become part of a community.

It wasn't until later, though, that I fully appreciated the lesson my parents taught me. When you refuse to quit, you give yourself the chance to learn about yourself and to discover new talents you didn't know you had. When you start and end the season as a team, win or lose, you finish the season together. There is no "I" in the word "team." As a team, you are a part of something bigger than just yourself, and whether you believe it or not, everyone is important to the team.

Believe me, these childhood experiences definitely contributed to one of my strengths – never giving up.

Looking back, I see how important that strength was to have, particularly when things got tough socially and academically later on during my journey.

"*He will never
be on the straight
and narrow;
but it's been
a great journey
on the wide and curvy.*"

— PELE CHILDRESS, MOM OF ADHD CHILD

4

The Swing

I feel sad when I think about the many challenges I experienced during elementary school.

I absolutely dreaded school.

Let me be clear that it wasn't *my* school that I found so distressing… I hated *any* school.

School work and sitting through class was difficult no matter what school I attended.

I loved my friends, I loved wearing a uniform, I loved the campus, and I liked the teachers. It was sitting through class and the actual school-work that I despised and found so daunting.

I was successful with homework and projects outside of school because frequent breaks and space available for organization assisted in my success. There were few distractions at home and

I had ample space to spread out my assignments
and unlimited time for frequent breaks. My grades
were consistently excellent on assignments
completed outside of the classroom.

In 6th grade, I remember working on a "Flags
of the United States" social studies project. This
project was intimidating, as there were many
flags to create and states to research. I was sure
it would be cumbersome and exhausting to
complete, so I put it off for a while. Finally, when
I sat down to attack the project, I realized something so fascinating. After completing the first
state flag's history, I stood up, turned the clock
radio on, and danced around my room for a few
minutes. When the song was over, I turned the
radio off and sat down at my white wicker desk
with an unusually clear mind. So I continued on
with another state flag. I finished the second flag,
got up and turned on the radio again, danced
around my room, and so on.

I experienced a clear mind and renewed
ability to focus after dancing around for a few
minutes. It was almost like I had little bursts of
concentration, feeling more awake following
movement and distraction. I was able to crank
out the flag project in no time, as I had frequent

breaks, wasn't rushed, and had ample time to refocus. As a result, I received an A on the United States Flag project ... and, I must add, the teacher wrote "well done" on the top of the project. This was a great feeling of success. ***Only I*** knew the strange idiosyncrasies and routine that occurred — dancing around to music 50 times — that led to this achievement of an A on a significant part of the semester grade.

As early as elementary school, I knew I learned differently compared to the other students.

I just HAD to learn differently... as no one looked as stressed out or as lost while completing a simple reading and comprehension assignment.

Reading comprehension is nearly impossible for a student with no focus, who has a foggy mind, and is unable to sit still for more than five minutes. Reading comprehension assignments for an unfocused student are equivalent to someone reading a bunch of words on a page and having no idea what they just read. The inattentive reader absorbs little or nothing. An inattentive reader is able to regurgitate the main character of story's first name, but not able to tell you anything else about what they just read. It is such a challenge to explain, and especially understand, if you don't experience it first-hand.

No one else stared at a tree outside the window for the entire class. I almost think it's unfair to put windows in classrooms because the windows made it so easy to daydream and escape what was essentially hour upon hour of lost time. Actually, I think I had a love-hate relationship with the windows in the classroom. I loved looking outside and drifting off to another place, while at the same time, hating the distraction they provided because of the trouble my daydreaming caused.

I remember looking outside the windows of my classroom in elementary school, watching the groundskeepers with the landscaping and wishing I was them. I wanted to have their job, a simple job that took me outside and away from the classroom. The custodial staff "got to move around and do stuff like cleaning, and taking out trash," and I thought they were so lucky. I wanted to be anywhere but in that classroom.

Headaches were frequent and unwelcome visitors as I was overcome with worry about each school day. The anxiety crept in at 0730 with morning carpool, continuing to the first 'work' of the day. Next, I would worry about which math group I would be assigned, followed by worry about getting another "D" with the words "careless, redo, or please finish your answer" written in red pen all over the paper. Unbeknown to the teacher, her negative feedback contributed to the pre-existing negative feelings I had about myself. The school day even ended with worry — worry about the homework assigned for that evening.

The angst was constant, although it varied throughout the day. After school, I feared my parents would be disappointed with me about my poor grades. Our parents never punished us for bad grades, but they could not hide their disappointment, as they knew I worked very hard and **wanted** academic success. I imagine they probably felt more sad for me than disappointed.

I attended Oak Hill School, a prestigious, private, Catholic elementary school. We were required to wear uniforms.

I loved wearing the uniform because we all looked the same.

I secretly hoped that my classmates and teachers wouldn't realize how distracted I was if we all looked the same.

Another reason I liked wearing a uniform was that at least I would **look** organized and put together, even if I didn't feel that way.

My brogue shoes were always polished, skirt pleats ironed, and oxford shirt neatly pressed. In retrospect, I think these obsessive behaviors related to underlying OCD, one of the comorbid conditions that exist in individuals with ADHD.

I was hopeful that my clean and polished outer appearance would boost my confidence inside, and it did… maybe a little. I also hoped that I looked like everyone else on the surface, especially the perceived smart students.

In the classroom, we were placed into three groups: A, B or C (the teachers said it had nothing to do with academic aptitude, but I disagree). I was **always** in the C group — the group with the students needing frequent remediation.

Such academic segregation has the potential to adversely affect kids, and it definitely affected me. I felt stupid in the C group.

In addition to being distracted and unfocused, I was also extremely impulsive in elementary school. The most significant impulsive incident occurred when I was in First Grade.

My best friend Liza and I were running to

recess to swing, as we always did. Unfortunately, when we arrived on the playground, only one of the five swings was available. My best friend hopped up onto the last remaining swing and started happily pumping away as I stood there, angrily. At that very moment, I noticed a new girl swinging on the end of the swing set. She was new to our class, and I asked, "May I please have a turn?"

"No," She replied.

I stood with my arms crossed, huffing, puffing, leaning on the swing set, acting annoyed, until I asked her nicely a second time to use the swing, and again she said, "No."

Impulsively, without thinking, without caring, I hauled off and slapped her across the face. She fell backwards from the swing and started crying.

I felt terrible about slapping her for a moment, but then I jumped up onto that swing and started pumping my legs happily.

All was great in my world until the teacher asked us what happened and I got into big trouble.

Off the swing I went and straight into the principal's office.

They called my mom and she was shocked, angry, and disappointed. My parents were baffled and could not understand where this impulsive behavior came from, as we never hit in our household and we certainly didn't hit to solve problems.

Regardless, I struck a fellow first grader and had to be punished. I felt bad about the situation, suffered consequences at home, and lost recess for a week at school. I wrote the student a note to apologize and never struck anyone again.

This was the first major sign of my impulsivity, and a clear example of the 'quickness to anger' that Dr. Hallowell describes in children with ADHD.

"Thank God, for recess, art and gym," was my mantra throughout the day. It is pretty obvious why I loved those diversions, and sadly, it was the only part of the school day I enjoyed.

ADHD students thrive during recess, PE and Art, as those hours provide students the ability to move around, self-express, and not feel the ever present academic segregation.

"When you can't stand it anymore, get on your knees and pray."

— SUSAN KOVACS, MSW

5

Daydream Believer

Many individuals with ADHD are creative, imaginative, and verbal, and it is important for parents and educators to recognize these qualities and provide outlets for further development.

During my second grade parent-teacher conference, my teachers discussed "what a significant daydreamer I was and how inattentive I was" during the school day.

The morning was always better for concentration, but it was short lived as I would soon drift off into space or begin doodling on worksheets. There were days that I would be a million miles away… thinking about riding bikes with my friend after school or what we were having for dinner. Without warning, the teacher would call on me for the answer to a question she had just asked the class. I would snap out of my far-away place, not knowing the answer as I had no idea what the class was talking about. Not only did I feel stupid, but I was also angry with myself for being distracted again, not to mention humiliated in front of my peers.

Daydreaming and inattentiveness started as early as second grade and continued throughout high school. I was frustrated, angry, and annoyed that my brain would not allow me to pay attention for more than just a few minutes at a time.

I could not even pretend to know what was going on in class. The sad part was, I truly could not help it.

I wish I had been able to express to my parents and teachers how much I wanted to do well in elementary school. Yet even though I didn't have the words, my parents must have known how badly I wanted to succeed, and they never gave up in their support of me. Tutors were hired, and I attended learning centers and summer school.

I was a 'pleaser' and wanted to please everyone including my parents, my teachers, **and** myself.

It isn't that students with ADHD don't want to participate or want to daydream. They truly are unable to control their focus or attentiveness.

It is nearly impossible to make your brain focus and remember things when it just can't, due to a biochemical imbalance. The attempt to focus and not be able to results in an overwhelming sense of failure.

Feeling like a failure leads to low self-esteem, and ultimately, poor grades.

I remember thinking that the letter grade assigned to a group, or the grade on a test, was equivalent to a label for a student. Meaning, an A for a smart student, a B for a good student, and so on. Even though my parents made me feel like a C was okay, I always wanted to do better — for me, not them — because I just didn't feel that I was intelligent enough.

Punctuality was never my issue. I was never late for school. I turned in homework neatly and on time, and the day usually started out pretty well.

However by mid-morning my spacey inattentiveness would kick in. Almost habitually,

I would not know what page we were on, and when called on would fail to answer the question appropriately. This cycle continued for years during elementary school, and led to an almost self-loathing existence — married with a severely deflated self-confidence. Despite teacher reassurance telling me, "We know you are trying your best, but just try to pay attention during class," and, "a C is fine." It was not fine.

I was miserable and my doubt consumed me. I felt like I would never get through school, and never become a nurse.

As I got older, paranoia began to take root. I thought the other students were talking about me because of my lack of attention. I worried other girls would not like me because I sometimes got them in trouble. My asking what page we were on led to them sharing the answer, and according to the teacher, disrupting the class. So at this point, not only was I zoning out during class — not participating and daydreaming — but also was being disruptive — talking while trying to figure out what question had just been asked. The more the cycle continued, the worse I felt.

I envied the kids who paid attention and I wanted to be like them. I wanted to be able to focus on the curriculum and participate. However, no matter how hard I tried, how early I went to bed the night before, or maintained a routine, I drifted off in space within minutes of being in the classroom.

One of my seventh grade teachers did not like me at **ALL**. I think it was because of my lack of participation and inattentiveness during her class. I knew how much she could not stand me by the way I felt she looked at me and picked on me for **everything**.

I mentioned it to my parents, and they began to believe that this teacher did not like me — which may have been partially justified, maybe — **BUT** she still needed to be professional and treat me with respect in the classroom.

My parents always reminded us that life is not fair and people will not always like you, but even if that is the case, you need to be kind to others.

This teacher was not kind or respectful to me during class *or* anytime. In fact, she made snide comments about me under her breath and wrote in red pen all over my tests in massive capital letters: "REDO" or "CARELESS!"

My seventh grade history classroom at Villa Duchesne *(see photos in appendix)* was large, with massive tall windows on two of the three walls, a blackboard in front of the classroom, and an overhead projector. We didn't have PowerPoint or Smart Boards in 1987. I was always on time for history class, sat in the front or middle row, and tried to focus on the lesson. Despite my constant struggle with my mind to stay focused, I was rarely able to fully pay attention, resulting in day dreaming and fidgeting — which drove this teacher crazy.

One afternoon while sitting in her class, spacey as usual, I was turning my earring round and round in my ear without a care in the world. I was daydreaming and totally unaware of how much my twisting and turning of an earring post upset my teacher. Exasperated at my transgression, she stopped teaching, and in front of my class-mates, very loudly, asked me to stop. Mortified, I immediately stopped turning my earring, paid attention, and remained focused for about 15 minutes. And then, the inattentiveness took hold and I started twisting my earring again, completely oblivious that I was doing so. It was an impulsive behavior rather than an act of defiance.

I was not trying to be difficult.

I was not talking or being disruptive; it was

just a nervous habit.

My teacher freaked out and yelled, "KRISTIN, STOP IT RIGHT NOW! GO TO SISTER CAIRE'S OFFICE!" With that, she sent me out of class and straight to the principal's office. Ironically, the principal was just as perplexed as I was as to why my teacher punished me for turning my earring. Nevertheless, I served my punishment and sat in Sister Caire's office for the duration of class, and then went home as usual.

Later that evening I told my mom what happened. She was perturbed with the teacher for coming down so hard on me and embarrassing me, and didn't think the punishment fit the crime.

That night, my teacher called my parents and said, "You won't believe what Kristin did today." My parents were concerned and wondered what I must have **really** done — it must have been far worse that what I shared earlier that evening. Long story short, the teacher shared that I twisted my earring throughout class and didn't stop upon her request. She explained that it was distracting for her while she was teaching her lesson. My parents listened quietly, and I listened outside my parents' bedroom door hearing only their end of the conversation. I had to silence my gasp when

I heard my mom's response.

"Please let me clarify the circumstances that occurred today during class so that we understand why you are calling us... Kristin quietly twisted her earring during class and you found this to be disruptive behavior. That resulted in Kristin being humiliated by you yelling at her, and then you sent her to the principal's office?"

The teacher stood by her convictions and I assume replied, "Yes, that is what happened."

My mom finished the conversation with, "Lady, you need a vacation!" and hung up the phone.

I will never forget that day because I knew then that my parents had my back.

They knew I tried my best in school and they empathized with how difficult it was for me to focus and pay attention. This particular teacher was kicking me while I was down, which was not okay with my parents, and my mom let her know. For this I was grateful, and almost felt relief. I felt relieved that my mom stuck up for me with the ridiculous humiliation in class and pathetic call home that night. I was relieved that, although I could be distracted and disruptive, I truly was not in this instance.

This teacher could not stand me. I am confident that she thought I was a spoiled brat who was disrespectful in her class. The fact is that she was trapped in her own spiral of misery. She was going through personal difficulties, and unfortunately, took her troubles out on me. I later realized there was an underlying reason for this madness, but back in seventh grade social studies class, I felt like she hated me. She was ready to pounce, and quick to humiliate me. The earring example is un-exaggerated and took place during a bad time in this woman's life. It really goes to show that sometimes the front we try to portray on the outside can't cover up what's really going on inside — such as this history teacher's personal issues that were projected onto me in seventh grade.

This treatment was very unusual from the teachers at my school. Most them worked tirelessly to support all students. They were dedicated and committed to helping their students achieve academic success, as well as confidence. There were many times that my math and science teachers met with me before or after school, on their own time, to assist me with understanding the subject matter being taught. They knew that

I wanted to do well, they noticed my desire to learn, and they saw that I tried to apply myself. They would invest hours of their time to help me. If I tried, they tried. Thus, they were willing to invest in me. The teacher who yelled at me for twisting my earring was definitely not the norm at Villa Duchesne, but nonetheless, she left quite a negative imprint on me.

In the end, I passed her class with a C, and I made extra effort to give her the respect she deserved as a teacher. I managed to finish the year without any further outbursts from her or being humiliated by her again, and, thankfully, never had her as a teacher again.

My biology teacher, Mr. Littlefield was quite the opposite of my seventh grade history teacher. He saw the fierce determination in my eyes and my driven spirit. He was an outstanding teacher who had a tremendous influence on virtually all his students. Mr. Littlefield made such an impression on me and had a huge impact on my future — he ignited the spark in my love of learning science. Everything about him from his blue lab coat he wore during class, to his commanding voice, reeled me in right away. I told him I was going to be a nurse someday.

He recognized and appreciated my commitment and he worked as hard as I did to help me achieve a B in Biology.

Mr. Littlefield knew I spent my summers taking summer school classes and volunteering at local nursing homes as a candy striper. I loved the elderly. I volunteered at Marie de Ville and St. John's skilled nursing home for four summers. He knew the value I felt when taking care of people and my desire to become a nurse. I voiced these things to him when he was helping me study before and after class. Mr. Littlefield actually believed I would indeed **BE** a nurse someday. I clearly found value in myself, and understood that other people valued me, too, when I took care of them.

The residents at the nursing home loved when I would visit their room, read the paper to them, or help them eat. I felt so happy — and good about myself — when I was able to meet the residents' needs and bring them comfort.

"Just try to stay focused through science class, even if it is just for today," I would bargain with myself. I used to tell myself that if I participated during class and was not caught daydreaming or doodling, that maybe I could take an extra bike ride after school. This bartering didn't work and

I could not even pretend to be engaged in school.

Students at Villa Duchesne, the Catholic school I attended, were required to attend weekly mass on Thursday mornings beginning in first grade. As long as I can remember, I would pray for the ability to be smart.

I would pray and ask God to "please make me smart, able to concentrate, and not get into trouble in school." I never felt that my prayers were answered, but I still kept the faith and kept trying.

"You can never
cross the ocean
until you have
the courage to lose sight
of the shore."

— CHRISTOPHER COLUMBUS

6

Memory Lane

No one understood that the inattentiveness and impulsiveness were beyond my control.

I wanted to do a good job and produce solid work. It was frustrating for my parents and teachers, but more frustrating for me.

I was surviving, not excelling, academically.

Occasionally I had the correct answer to a question asked, but unfortunately, I blurted it out without being called on, which was a problem.

Other times, I would raise my hand before the teacher finished asking the entire question. Then when she called on me, I didn't know the right answer as I only heard **part** of the question. These are examples of classic ADHD traits occurring in the classroom.

I struggled with impulsive tendencies at home and in school because I wanted to appear "smart" and actively participate. Unfortunately, I too often "jumped the gun" with my desire. It is difficult to express well in words what it is like to be impulsive. Very rarely do you realize it before you can get out of your own way.

Maybe it was age, maybe it was self-doubt, maybe it was even a bit of envy, but one of the biggest reasons for me beating myself up over my perceived failures was because I saw what I wanted every day of my life. It did not help my psyche that one person I looked up to more than most seemed to have everything I did not.

My sister has always been extremely bright and academically inclined. She didn't have to work very hard in school in order to achieve straight A's. We are two years apart to the day, and — as is common with many sister relationships — were best friends as little kids, hated each other, then loved each other and were best friends again.

There were many nights I would lie next to my sister after she was asleep and pray for osmosis, telepathy, or really anything to get her brain cells into my head.

One night in fourth grade, while lying next to her as she slept in her blue and white bedroom, I remember thinking, *'Is it the way she breathes or sleeps that makes her remember everything and be so smart? What is it? Why can't I have this peace, restful sleep, and good grades?'*

I was so sad. I still remember to this day lying there and wishing to be like her.

I wanted her brain. Things came so easy for her and that made me angry. Why did I have to work so hard for a C and she could achieve A's with little effort?

We had the same parents, the same rules, and attended the same school, but I struggled so much more than my sister. I resented her because school seemed so easy for her.

The anger I felt as a result of poor grades was obvious when I recently read an old note that I had passed to a friend in middle school.

My friend, Liza, shared an entire bag of our notes she kept from 25 years ago that we had passed to one another during class — example of me not paying attention. Reading the notes was like a Technicolor trip down memory lane.

Several notes were mundane and boring, but some were really funny. We were laughing out loud reliving our shared bits of history written so many years ago.

And then, in an instant, everything changed. One note in particular was very telling of my undiagnosed ADHD, and I found it very sad.

The note described a fight I had with my sister the night before and provided insight to my scattered thoughts and inattentiveness, as well as anger and resentment towards her.

My feelings of frustration at the time were as obvious as neon lights when I read the note. I freely scribed curse words and mean comments about my sister and about our fight the night before. I wrote about the punishment — my parents taking my "phone" privileges away — because I had scratched my sister and was being awful to her. I was so furious that I could not call my friend as planned, and blamed my sister for telling my parents and getting me in trouble.

The story then shifted from the fight with my sister, to weekend plans with friends, to what I was wearing that weekend, to who was pretty, to asking what page we were on in class. The thoughts were scattered and my aggravation was transparent.

Retrospectively, it was at best, a subconscious

flirtation with a perception of failure. But in reality, the girl in that note knew all too well that not only was she thoroughly disappointing herself, but also, she was utterly frustrated that she lacked the ability to figure out why.

The affect that undiagnosed ADHD had on my life was clearly visible in the old note — my chicken scratch handwriting, thoughts shifting from topic to topic, and "quick to anger" behavior.

This rare insight into my past also made me recognize my lack of self-love.

I reflected for a moment and thought, *'If I could reach out and share my story — my experience with ADHD and the vicious cycle of anxiety, distractibility, and impulsiveness which resulted in an overall poor self-image — maybe I could offer some perspective for someone.'*

I realized, maybe I could share insight that might help someone help their child with ADHD – or help themselves.

Maybe I could reassure someone who's child is struggling with ADHD that ***it is possible to get through the fog***... their child ***can*** grow up and live a productive, successful, happy life.

*"The most
difficult thing
is the decision to act,
the rest
is merely tenacity."*

— AMELIA EARHART

7

Pieces of the Puzzle

Comorbidities are commonly associated with attention-deficit hyperactivity disorder (ADHD) in children, adolescents, and adults.

The expert clinician, the parents, and the teachers need to ask themselves, "Does this person have ADHD, ADHD plus another condition, or is it another psychiatric condition altogether masquerading as ADHD?"

This is an important component of the diagnostic process that requires medical and psychological evaluation to definitively rule out other diagnoses.

Since little was known in the 1980's about ADHD, my parents requested a re-evaluation by another reading specialist for other possible Learning Disabilities (LD) such as dyslexia. Nothing ever resulted from this evaluation, which aggravated my parents, teachers, and especially me. I was referred to as "an inattentive and careless student."

As I look back, I now realize that I was one of the earliest pioneers of this condition, ADD/ADHD. With so little known at the time of my struggling and subsequent evaluation, I was left hanging with no confirmed diagnosis or plan.

In retrospect, there is no doubt that I had ADHD, with an underlying mild anxiety that manifested itself through OCD tendencies, and later, some mild depression.

The #1 comorbid condition that exists with ADHD is Oppositional Defiance Disorder and it is found in approximately 48% of children with ADHD *(American Academy of Child and Adolescent Psychiatry, 2009)*. Oppositional Defiance Disorder is defined by the American Academy of Child and Adolescent Psychiatry as "an ongoing pattern of uncooperative, defiant, and hostile behavior toward authority figures that seriously interferes with the youngster's day-to-day functioning."

Studies suggest that up to 16% of **ALL** school aged children and adolescents have ODD. The causes of ODD are unknown, but many parents reported that "their child with ODD was more rigid and demanding than the child's siblings, and signs were evident at an early age. Biological, psychological, and social factors may have a role" *(AACP, 2009)*. Symptoms include temper tantrums, wanting to seek revenge, and purposely not obeying rules or respecting authority figures. To be clear: this defiance is an intentional behavior.

The next most common ADHD co-existing condition is Conduct Disorder, followed by Anxiety, OCD, Coordination Problems, and Depression. There were times I felt like I had all of these conditions in addition to ADHD.

Specifically speaking to the OCD tendencies, I remember my ***obsession*** with the TV commercial "Coke is it!" in 1988. The people were happy, dancing to a quip melody. I became physically giddy viewing the commercial, singing along. It was an instantaneous journey to my happy place.

During my 30 minutes of television time one night I flipped through the channels until I found the Coca-Cola commercial. Back in my youth, there was no YouTube or TiVo, so I sat watching various stations and changing channels until I found the coveted commercial. Once I heard it, I obsessively wrote the lyrics down word for word, and even noted the high and low pitches with music notes penned on a notecard. It lived on my bedside table, and I would study it again and again before going to sleep. The next morning I took the note card and started singing (silently in my head), "Coke is it!" just like the commercial. For some reason, this decreased my anxiety and I found myself in a better mood when I sang or heard that song. Never before would I have recognized that this was an example of obsessive behavior, but it clearly was such a manifestation. The jingle and lyrics from that commercial somehow decreased my angst before school and made me feel good inside.

I was obsessed with routines, songs, and various idiosyncrasies like not stepping on cracks in the driveway.

I was consumed with being organized, and later realized this drive for organization stemmed from a need for order: the structure I required to feel successful.

My school uniform was another example of possible underlying OCD and the need to appear organized. The uniform skirt had to have perfectly ironed pleats, shoes polished, turtleneck tight around the neck, and matching socks. By matching socks, I mean the brand, the color, and the height of the two socks had to be exactly the same.

Another example of underlying OCD, anxiety and the need to fit in with my peers, is when I wanted to change my name from Kristin to Kristy. Ninety percent of my classmates were named Corey, Susie, Molly, Amy, Winnie, Katie, Kelly, Julie and Jenny. Nearly everyone's name ended in a 'y' or 'ie' and I always hated being Kristin. My best friend, Liza, had a unique name too, which also probably was a reason we bonded the first day of first grade. Nevertheless, my parents refused to let me change my name. They loved that I was Kristin and they were sticking to it. In hindsight, I am proud and glad I had a unique name in elementary and high school.

I had to be early to everything. It was enough to ruin my entire day if I was late to anything. One of my mottos is, "If you're not five minutes early, you're late."

Being on time, neat, and organized, gave me security in the arenas where I was afraid of being thought of as insufficient... or worse, insignificant.

Despite having three other children, my parents

did their best to accommodate my need to be early to everything while arriving with clean, pressed, and matching attire.

They assisted me with controlling the things we were able to control — such as arrival times, outfits, meals and carpool mates — as it was calming and provided order and structure in my day.

The most infamous obsession was having complete and total silence at bedtime.

Falling asleep was a challenge for me all throughout elementary, middle, and high school.

Despite consuming a diet low in sugar and caffeine, and getting physical exercise, I was not able to "calm my brain" enough to fall asleep. I would lay in bed, reeling over something said that day that bothered me, or what I needed to do the next morning, or simply being fixated on the fact that I could not fall asleep.

Regardless of why, I was unable to calm distractions or thoughts and peacefully drift off to sleep. It was a particularly aggravating dichotomy as I was physically exhausted.

I turned to God and prayed. I told Him how frustrated I was and would say, "Please help me fall asleep and start good and fresh in the morning."

I tried everything to fall asleep from counting flowers on the wallpaper, to walking around my bedroom making sure that everything was neat and organized, to adjusting my shades so the street light could not shine through the side crack, ensuring the room was pitch black. Despite all of my efforts, I still could not sleep. The digital clock changed from hour to hour, and the later it was, the more anxious I became.

I remember jumping out of bed yelling, "Shut-Up! I am trying to sleep!" at my siblings who ran down the staircase too loudly, took a late evening shower, or flushed the toilet in our shared Jack-N-Jill bathroom.

Dr. Hallowell describes these behaviors as "rage reactions." Individuals suffering from ADHD are often quicker to anger than those individuals without ADHD.

With respect to my need for silence at bedtime, the flushing toilet exacerbated the "noise" in my brain, eliciting an enraged reaction of yelling at my siblings. I knew that once awakened, I would have to start the ritual of "calming my brain down" all over again.

My parents dined together late in the evening, and I would frequently visit them downstairs and tell them how I could not sleep. Usually, they would try to talk to me or let me stay up with them for a little while and then I would head back up to bed. Sometimes it worked, but often I just lied in my bed, awake for hours.

It was a vicious cycle; with no sleep, I was more distracted and inattentive during the school day.

This frustrating merry-go-round was the result of an overactive brain and the lack of appropriate neurotransmitter communication.

Today, most physicians inquire about sleep patterns during assessments of patients displaying symptoms of ADHD. In fact, it is one of the first questions asked during the initial evaluation. It is a significant piece of the puzzle and helpful in obtaining an accurate diagnosis of ADHD. My example illustrates why, with an active mind, it can be difficult to calm the brain and fall asleep.

Elementary school principals, teachers, and parents ask me about ADHD testing, as they are curious about what should be involved in the diagnostic process of evaluating a child for possible ADHD, and who should be trusted to make the correct diagnosis.

The distractibility associated with ADHD stems from an underlying neurotransmitter communication in the brain. This predominantly neurological condition needs to be addressed by the student's parents, teachers, and a team of medical professionals.

The ADHD brain has less naturally occurring Dopamine, Norepinephrine (NE) and Serotonin. These neurohormones are balanced in the non ADHD frontal and parietal lobes, enabling a person without ADHD to focus, maintain attention, be more alert and decisive. The lack of Dopamine, NE and Serotonin in the ADHD brain, results in an unfocused, irritable, hyperactive, inattentive, and impulsive individual. Although it seems paradoxical to administer a stimulant medication to an already impulsive and 'hyperactive' person, this class of medication drastically improves and 'normalizes' or balances the neurohormones resulting in a clearer, more focused, less impulsive state of mind.

Based on my first-hand experience as a patient, an ideal place to start is with the child's pediatrician. Once they are on the same page and agree that ADHD symptoms are present, it could be beneficial to include a psychiatrist, the child's teachers and coaches. The multidisciplinary team will assess the child in a holistic manner, then provide insight and share information to carefully determine the presence of ADHD. The clinicians will collaborate with parents, teachers and coaches to create a mutually agreed upon individualized care plan. It is important that *everyone* (especially the child!) agrees on the plan. If there is no commitment from the child being treated (if they are old enough and able to understand and cooperate), they will not be successful. The last thing anyone wants is for the student to feel additional failure, so he or she must be engaged and committed to the plan.

And no matter what, whether or not prescription medication is prescribed, this is a long-haul effort. ***There is no overnight miracle cure.***

Many pediatricians conclude a child has ADHD based on a teacher's one-time note or a parent's voiced frustration. It is disheartening when parents fail to consult all available experts and resources and rely solely on one person's assessment and diagnosis of ADHD, which can ***sometimes*** be inconclusive or inaccurate.

I know that I was fortunate to have an incredible support system and the financial resources to aid me at school and during my evaluation. I fully recognize that few people are able to tap into such resources and testing (to be discussed later). However, the resources available within the public school system and through various support groups such as CHADD (Children and Adults with ADHD) Foundation are abundant. The public and private school systems have counselors, therapists, teachers and resource rooms available and are committed to helping all students, including those with ADHD.

Parents, teachers, coaches, therapists, counselors, and physicians, working together as a team, can best determine an accurate diagnosis while taking into account the child's health history, a physical exam, school records, and possibly, a sleep study. Upon diagnosis, it is important to consider the impact of administering to a child a schedule II medication that could have detrimental effects if not monitored by an experienced clinician.

> Schedule II drugs, substances, or chemicals are defined as drugs with a high potential for abuse, with use potentially leading to severe psychological or physical dependence. These drugs are also considered dangerous. Some examples of Schedule II drugs are: (Vicodin), cocaine, methamphetamine, methadone, hydromophone (Dilaudid), meperidine (Demerol), oxycodone (OxyContin), fentanyl, Dexedrine,

Adderall, and Ritalin. *(United States DEA – Drug Enforcement Administration dea.gov)*

It is crucial to try other non-pharmacological measures prior to trying medications, as they have the potential to be abused and mismanaged **IF** not prescribed with a comprehensive workup, and by a reputable and responsible physician.

> "When medication works, it works as safely and dramatically as eyeglasses. Medication helps about 80% of the time in the treatment of ADHD. Make sure you work with a doctor who can explain the issues around medication to you clearly. Most people do not realize how safe and effective stimulant medications truly are, when they are used properly. Make sure you work with a doctor who has plenty of experience with these medications. The stimulants include medications like Ritalin, Concerta, Adderall, Vyvanse, Focalin, and others. As long as you take them under proper medical supervision, they can help immensely." *(From an interview of Dr. Hallowell in a Psychology Today Podcast)*

According to Hallowell, general pediatricians receive about three to five credit hours of pediatric assessment, diagnosis, treatment, and pharmacology for ADHD while in medical school. Pediatricians are required to know a lot about everything regarding all pediatric medical conditions, and most have a wealth of knowledge that is considered fairly all-encompassing.

Today, pediatricians and family practitioners are often responsible for identifying the presence of ADD/ADHD in an individual. Not everyone has the resources available in their community to consult a pediatric neurologist or psychiatrist. Alternatively, the family physician or pediatrician is an excellent and qualified resource to diagnose the child, and work with parents/guardians and teachers to develop a proper medication regimen if indicated. Psychologists and counselors provide the necessary insight and talk therapy to assist the pediatricians in diagnosing ADHD and formulating a care plan. The collaboration and cooperation of psychologists, physicians, parents and teachers is essential in the success of the care plan. Just as important is ongoing communication of the effects of medication and other interventions on the patient. When there is a question regarding what medication is best after several trials of different medications, or if the pediatrician is not comfortable prescribing stimulants or scheduled medication, a pediatric neurologist or psychiatrist should be consulted.

*"The harder
the struggle,
the more glorious
the triumph."*

— Swami Sivananda

8

Ball Dropped

In fourth grade, things at school were not getting better — they were getting worse — and so were the headaches.

My parents decided to have me tested by a "highly regarded education expert and reading specialist."

My parents, teachers, pediatrician, and I were all hopeful that the test results and subsequent assessment would provide an answer to the cause of my inattentiveness and poor academic performance. More importantly, we were eager to find the tools available to assist with my struggle.

The PhD noted my IQ to be "significantly above average," and found no clinical reason (dyslexia, poor IQ, or LD) to explain my poor grades or performance in school.

Unfortunately, this highly regarded education expert and reading specialist **missed critical indicators** that would have led her to an accurate diagnosis of ADHD.

It is important to remember that ADHD was still being actively researched during this time, and little was known about the condition. In fact, the earliest papers describing neurotransmitter communication and defining ADHD were published in 1983 and 1984. Ironically, this was around the same time I was tested.

As a result of the education expert's failure to identify or understand key indicators that would have led to a diagnosis of ADHD, the results of the tests were inconclusive. The evaluator chalked up my behavior to be "the result of being distracted and inattentive." Her recommendations: "tutoring and counseling."

I remained impulsive (and still do today) and can remember another vivid example of reactive impulsivity when my baby brother was born. This is a classic example of impulsive ADHD behavior in a 10 year old.

My brother was born around midnight in December of 1982. Karen, Scott and I were at home with a babysitter eagerly awaiting the call

from my parents from the hospital. The minute
I heard the phone ring, I knew it had to be my
parents letting us know we had a new sibling. I
jumped out of bed and answered the phone, spoke
with them briefly then hung up the phone. Instead
of going back to bed as Karen, Scott and the sitter
had done, I could not wait to tell the world about
John Paul's arrival. So, I pulled out the buzz books
from my Mom's dresser and began calling every
single person with the news. I remember waking
people up all night until finally, at about 1:30am,
one of my Mom's good friends said, "Kristin
honey, this is exciting news but couldn't it wait
until the morning?" I was impulsive and excited.
I wanted to immediately share this happy news.
I did not realize that my calling and waking
people in the middle of the night would be so
intrusive and truly could have waited.

Further evaluation and consultation with
a pediatric neurologist occurred much later
in my academic career in 1991, while a freshman
in college.

To this day, my mom says that one of her
biggest regrets was not having me re-tested in
high school. Honestly, hindsight is 20-20 and
that's why we have it — to learn from it. Without

question, in my eyes, she should have not an ounce of regret as they did everything possible to try to help me.

Following the IQ and LD testing performed in fourth grade, my parents took me to visit several different middle schools. They wanted to be certain that *I wanted* to stay at the challenging school where I was enrolled. They wanted to give me the opportunity to visit other schools — to see what other options were available to me. We knew the school work would only get more difficult in the years to come.

After visiting the schools, I was *positive* I wanted to stay where my friends were. I remember visiting one of the private schools and noticing that their ninth grade science textbook was the same textbook we were using at my current school in the seventh grade. I thought, *'If I want to be a nurse I must be good in science. I will also get a better college prep education if I stay where I am.'*

My school had an impressive science lab that offered hands-on learning from world class teachers.

We made the decision to stay at the school I attended. I was happy with my choice. But I knew that my school work, and my life, would only get harder.

*"If you obey
all the rules,
you miss all the fun."*

— KATHARINE HEPBURN

9

Class Clown

During middle school and high school, I developed a surge in impulsive and 'hyperactive' behavior.

This behavior was probably related to the normal homeostatic hormonal involvement of puberty, in addition to the underlying undiagnosed ADHD behaviors.

As a result, from seventh grade through my senior year, I used my sense of humor to be a "class clown." I was well liked by my peers and included in social events because I brought jokes and fun.

My high school experience was very different from that of the elementary school years. It was more fun, even though I had the same classmates, same school, and same stressors; I had a different, more jovial feeling inside.

The hyperactivity, commotion, and comedy I provided kept everyone laughing... except the faculty.

I loved science and was doing well in the subject. I had *finally* discovered a feeling of confidence with schoolwork. I continued to struggle in every other subject, so I continued to act out as a jokester because I felt appreciated by my classmates when I made them laugh. Part of it was the hunger for adulation; part of it was to mask my self-perceived inadequacy.

One example of this impulsive and hyperactive behavior was when I took all of the chalk and erasers from the Algebra teacher's chalkboard and hid them inside a desk where she could not find them. The whole class was laughing at the poor teacher. The teacher was embarrassed, frazzled, and ticked off. She never knew it was me who hid the erasers, but my friends and I knew. The teacher's lesson was delayed, and as a result we all fell behind... but hey, I was happy: 15 minutes less of agonizing classwork... and I made everyone laugh.

Another impulsive antic was when I attended school on Halloween dressed as a pregnant nun.

Yes, you read that correctly.

Keep in mind that I attended an all-girl Catholic school, run by nuns. As you might imagine, the nuns were **NOT** happy, and I spent that Thursday in detention. *Postscript: I even wrote "9 months" on a piece of paper and taped it to my stomach... not my smartest move.*

There were times I would stomp into a classroom already in session and distract others just to get attention, or belch loudly during lectures, or pass notes during class. Those are just a few examples of my impulsive and rude behavior exhibited during middle and high school.

Now that I better understand ADHD and am well versed on the condition, I view these behaviors as classic signs of someone with ADHD in desperate need of a plan.

When I was 15, I wrecked a car while taking driver education classes at the local high school. I was so excited to drive that I failed to turn sharp enough, and ran the car smack into a telephone pole about a mile from my neighborhood. As a result, I wasn't able to take the permit test until I was 16, and thus, received my driver's license at 17. The consequences of impulsivity and inattentiveness affected my life inside *and* outside of school.

I have always been a very capable individual and found ways to get around the rules.

I was out with my friends one weekend, and didn't want to come home for my curfew at 11 p.m. Our parents made us let them know we were home safely by waking them upon our return — they were usually waiting up anyway. At 10:30 p.m. one Saturday night, I knew my parents had to be asleep because they were up with my little brother the night before. I called my home phone number (no caller ID back then) and my mom answered the phone sleepily. I said, "Oh hey, mom, I got it," as if I was in my room on the other phone and had picked up the call the same time she did. My mom said, "You're home, okay great, good night." I was still out having a great time with my friends. I totally lied to my parents and purposely deceived them. Although that was a pretty clever way to stay at the party for another couple of hours, it was also manipulative. Smart, nonetheless, but sneaky.

My parents were smart as well. Resourceful, too. They even became friendly with the neighborhood Walgreens store cashier, Buffy. My mom and Buffy were on a first name basis when I was in high school. My mom asked Buffy to please notify her if we ever bought cigarettes, alcohol, or lots of toilet paper (for TP'ing) and gave Buffy our home phone number. I learned about their pact 25 years later when my mom shared the story with my friends... I always wondered how my mom knew when I was up to no good.

Looking back at the ways I compensated for low self-esteem — the result of poor grades and sometimes crippling insecurities — completely breaks my heart. I even picked up smoking in high school because it was 'cool' back then. Today I am better able to understand the reasons for my past behavior.

I found a way to turn what could have been a detriment into the very reason for many personal and professional successes.

But long before taking those final steps to any finish line, I had to keep getting up from every trip, stumble, and fall.

My metaphorical skinned knees and battle scars were constant reminders of my current reality. I had a tutor in **EVERY** subject except for art and gym. I even had a tutor in Theology!

No wonder I had deflated confidence! No wonder I tried to compensate in other ways! No wonder I felt the need to look great, be funny, attend every all boy high school dance, and always have a boyfriend!

In my eyes, those were the only areas — in addition to my inherent compassion for taking care of others — in which I excelled.

I had friends and was well-liked for the most part. My parents hosted weekend events such as pizza parties, sleepovers, and shopping trips. They recognized early on my need for fun, friendship, and acceptance. They helped me cultivate and maintain friendships that improved my self-confidence and psychosocial well-being. I cannot believe how hard my parents worked to keep me social, active, and well-liked by my peers. I invited other girls over to my house much more often than I was invited to their homes. I am sure they may have been embarrassed by my goofy behavior or drained from being with me at school.

Actually, 'exhausted' is probably the most fitting word I could use to describe how *anyone* must have felt after hanging out with me in high school.

I sought attention from others and needed constant reassurance that I was pretty, popular, or smart. I understand that most girls need reassurance, but typically that is given from parents and teachers. I needed it from parents, teachers, counselors, ***and*** my friends.

My parents planned parties and sleepovers that helped me stay connected and fostered my existing friendships — but never 'bought' my friends. I can't begin to imagine the effort it took or the sacrifices my parents made for me.

In addition to my girlfriends and the boys that were friends, or more than friends, I had one male friend in particular who was a source of support and a confidant during my high school years. I met him when I was 15 and we were close friends all through high school. He was always around to share a bite or catch a movie, and we went to school dances together if either one of us didn't have a boyfriend or girlfriend at the time to escort us. He was funny and positive and would pick me up when I was down.

However, like so many instances during that time, I could not get out of the way of my own bad behavior. I recently found a note that he wrote me when he was a freshman in college in 1991. It described a painful example of how I made an impulsive decision that hurt his feelings that year. According to the letter, he was so excited that I had invited him to my graduation dance. He was honored to be attending this special dance as one of my best friends, and so proud of my hard work and my upcoming graduation. Well, so much for me being a kind friend... I had invited someone else and, thus, uninvited my dear friend. I told him that I was sorry, but I had invited two people and he could not attend with me. ***How RUDE?!***

I cannot believe I committed such a mean, heartless act to my dedicated friend of five years! My insecurities and impulsiveness inflicted a deep wound to someone I would not hurt under almost any circumstance. I ended up going to my graduation dance with some random person who meant nothing to me, and deeply wounded my friend. I had forgotten about the whole situation, but stumbled across the old letter while organizing our storage room and writing this book.

Adolescents and young adults with ADHD may experience social, emotional, academic, and physical issues that impact quality of life, relationships, and success.

It is well documented how ADHD affects individuals psychosocially, and that working with a good therapist is helpful in achieving and maintaining successful relationships. If cost is an issue, one should utilize the school counselor, as all schools — both public and private — have counseling programs.

Counseling is essential for individuals of all ages with ADHD.

My parents found a speech therapist who worked with me occasionally. People could not understand a word I said. My speech was rapid, mumbled, and full of run-on sentences. As fast as the thoughts came, I would spit them out, resulting in garbled mumbo jumbo. People could not make heads or tails of what I was saying most of the time. Along with the rapid and unclear speech, I also experienced occasional stuttering. Thankfully, this speech pattern improved over the years with therapy. It is important to understand the speech component related to ADHD and seek support as needed. I was very fortunate to have parents who noticed I needed assistance and were able to provide the therapists and other resources necessary to help me succeed. However, resources are often available at no cost through the public school system for qualifying students.

My parents tried everything to help me be successful in school, sports, and even socially.

Unfortunately, I still felt like I was not good at much of anything other than taking care of people and being funny.

I had tutors for more hours than the hours I spent in the classroom. Can you imagine what that can do to one's self-esteem, especially when working so incredibly hard to achieve a mere C?

The high school years were a little better for me. Moving around to different classrooms was a godsend. I was able to sit, focus for a short time, then doodle or daydream. Before I knew it, boom: the bell would ring, the class was over, and we were off to another room. The physical movement from room to room and different setting in each classroom was a welcome and refreshing change for me.

I also liked the variety of teachers in high school. We had male and female teachers ranging from very experienced to novices. I loved most of them, as many of them tried to work with me, seemed to care about me, and even stayed late or came in early to assist me with understanding.

I LOVED BIOLOGY. As I mentioned earlier, my teacher was fantastic! He was a dynamic, hands-on instructor.

I loved Thursday because that was the one day we had 2 hours of science, including dedicated time in the laboratory. I thrived in this environment with the Bunsen Burners, petri dishes, and smell of formaldehyde, as well as the physical movement around the lab tables. Biology and Physics were my favorite classes during high school. I had wonderful teachers and lab partners, but most of all, I loved the information being taught.

There is that word again... Love.

Dr. Hallowell was right on when he described students with ADHD loving what they are doing or doing what they love — it is a recipe for success. This was true for me regarding science. Whether we were dissecting frogs in biology, making dry ice in chemistry, or demonstrating the laws of physics, I simply loved science.

For the first time in my life, I did not dread attending a class. This made me feel good about myself!

The love I experienced for science and my new desire to go to school was starting to give me hope... hope that my dream to be a nurse might actually become a reality. *"I just might get there,"* if I continue to love and understand science like this. I was finally happy at school.

Throughout high school, I participated in *Project Challenge.* It was an initiative that helped students who were not as academically inclined. Essentially, it was a group of C and D students who were paired up with more advanced, straight-A students. The A students volunteered to assist the C and D students to help them achieve better academic success. This was accomplished through peer tutoring and mentoring during lunch period on Wednesdays.

I liked *Project Challenge.* Although the name was awful, I liked working with a fellow classmate who wanted to see me succeed just as much as I wanted to succeed. We celebrated good results and grades and when I demonstrated good study skills. It helped me to get more organized and gain more confidence in my ability to study.

Project Challenge was a wonderful school sponsored program that fostered peer support, along with faculty support, in order to help students achieve better study skills and academic scores.

By the grace of God, the support of my parents, tutors, and teachers — *and my drive for success* —

I graduated high school *on time*, and *with no summer school needed after senior year*!! Graduating high school was one of the best feelings I had ever known.

I finally knew what it felt like to be genuinely proud of myself.

I remember that day like it was yesterday. My grandparents were at my graduation ceremony cheering me on, along with my siblings and proud parents. It was a special day that I will treasure forever. I knew how hard I worked to get that diploma.

We went out to dinner that night, and my dad made a toast regarding his pride in me and all my hard work. It was a moment in time that will be forever frozen in my memory, and my heart.

I was accepted to a few colleges on probation; in other words... under conditional acceptance. Nevertheless, I was accepted.

The first college acceptance letter came from Spring Hill College in Alabama. I was happy to be accepted to a college, especially one with such a gorgeous campus. The second college acceptance letter came from the University of Kansas, in

Lawrence. I was so excited to be accepted to two colleges that I could barely see straight.

I was elated — and was able to enjoy the *whole* summer before college — as **the summer of 1991 was the first summer of my ENTIRE academic career that I did not have to go to summer school**.

"It's not whether you get knocked down, it's whether you get up."

— VINCE LOMBARDI

10

Bad Decision
After Bad Decision

Against my parents' wishes, I chose to attend the University of Kansas.

It was an enormous campus with an enrollment of approximately 27,000 students. My parents were concerned about the size. They worried about the lack of structure associated with such a large institution. However, I couldn't wait to get the heck out of St. Louis and into a huge, co-ed university. I was ready to have a great time and start my nursing career.

My mom dropped me off at my dorm room, located in GSP Hall, in August of 1991. I was eager to experience all the good things college had to offer... maybe a little *too eager*. My impulsivity and lack of self-control was unbelievable...

It was like the old saying "a bat out of hell."

I was all over the map — figuratively and literally.

I almost never went to class, never took notes during class, and rarely turned in assignments.

Instead, I took road trips to see friends at other colleges, went out nightly, and even ventured on a last minute trip to go skiing in Colorado. I thought that being a Pi Kappa Alpha calendar girl and the Sigma Chi Derby Day Belching Queen (true story, unfortunately), was far more important than attending class. I barely made a 1.8 GPA (Grade Point Average) my first semester; second semester was pretty bad too, though not quite Blutarsky level. Regardless, I am confident my earned GPA was the result of attending only 12 lectures over the span of the entire year. I conned my parents into believing that I *really* was trying. I said, "college was just really hard," so they would let me stay and keep trying — or should I say, trying to find new and even more inventive ways to occupy my time with anything but studying.

My all-time bad, bad, **bad** decision was made during my freshman year at KU. I lied to my parents and took a road trip to attend a fraternity dance with an old high school boyfriend.

(Please keep in mind that my parents only allowed me to have a car during second semester because the campus was large and it got dark early in the evening. We agreed that I could have a car to get to and from classes safely.)

Upon granting me the use of a car — the red, convertible Toyota Celica, no less — for a few months to "safely" attend class, my parents made one important stipulation: I could not take the car anywhere out of state. There would be no road trips other than back to St. Louis for holidays.

Of course there wouldn't.

Not only did I *not* use the car to go to class, but I drove it out of state to Drake University in Iowa to attend the fraternity dance. My plan was to sneak back to KU without my parents knowing I had left. I sped along Interstate 35 without a care in the world, driving barefoot, smoking cigarettes, and littering along the way.

Suddenly, three police cars lined up ahead of me creating a barricade along the interstate with their lights flashing.

I stopped, as I pretty much had no choice since the highway was blocked, and faced the officer who asked for my license and registration.

Without thinking, I gave the officer my fake ID instead of my driver's license. He kept the fake ID, cited me for possession of a fake ID, and asked for my valid driver's license, which I handed over. The officer informed me that I was speeding — 95mph in a 65mph zone. He shared that a highway patrol helicopter flying overhead radioed the local police station to send the officers to stop me on I-35.

'This is just getting worse and worse,' I thought. The **second citation** I received was a speeding ticket. The helicopter also saw me littering. Thus, the **third citation** was for the big white McDonald's bag I had tossed out the window. The **fourth citation** was for driving barefoot and not wearing my seat belt.

The officer handed me the citations. The smart thing would have been to turn the car around and head back to KU. Guess what I did, instead? Bingo.

Most people would probably have turned around and gone home, but no, not this girl...

I was on a mission. I was ready to party. Drake is approximately 230 miles from Lawrence, Kansas — a four-hour drive from KU. I arrived safely, if not unscathed, to Drake and had a phenomenal time at the fraternity party.

I drove back to KU on Sunday afternoon following my fun, eventful weekend. I had just returned to my dorm room when my dad called.

"How was your weekend?" he asked.

"I studied the whole time," I lied. "It was so boring!" We made small talk and hung up.

About a month later, my dad opened the mail to find several ticket notices from Iowa that were the result of my infamous road trip. Whoops. I probably should have told him the truth a month ago because it only took seconds for my dad to put it all together: the date on the respective tickets, our phone conversation about my "studying all weekend," and my awful grades. I was caught in a bear trap with no feasible way to extricate myself.

He was furious that I lied to him. He was also furious that I took the car out of state — the one thing they asked me *NOT* to do. He called and told me that my mom was flying to Kansas City the next morning to drive the car back to St. Louis. He said that I could not be trusted and how disappointed they were in me and my poor choices.

I met my mom at the Kansas City airport and

handed over the car keys. We did not speak, and she could barely look me in the face. I knew she was livid. She got in the car and left, while I stood there — angry with myself and dumbfounded by what I had done.

I blew their trust and risked my own safety for some stupid party.

I rode the shuttle back to my dorm room from the airport, feeling terrible. I knew they were beyond angry and disappointed. For me to be so careless and impulsive, after all their help and support throughout elementary and high school, was utterly disheartening.

Now that I didn't have a car at KU, I had to figure out a way to get to important places like the mall, tanning salon and McDonald's. Forget class, I was so far behind the 8 ball that I didn't care. I felt worthless about school and clearly gave up — but didn't withdraw from classes, leaving me in a bigger mess. Nevertheless, I impulsively took, without permission, my roommate Veronica's new Honda Prelude to drive to the tanning salon. I figured since she was in class, she probably would not mind. *(Keep in mind, she never ok'd anyone using her car.)* I impulsively took her car keys and used the car without permission —

and without a care in the world. At 18 years old, you would think I would have waited for her to get out of class, then asked to use her car or asked for a ride. Nope, not this impulsive, hyperfocused girl... I was on a mission to tan. What happened? You guessed it! A car accident... I hit someone else's car in the parking lot of the tanning salon. Oh Great! JUST MY LUCK. Anyway, I felt bad briefly, but went in and tanned after the police officer wrote my ticket. This fender bender not only wrecked her car, it ruined our friendship. She was over it. She was over my antics and seemingly insensitive, impulsive behavior.

I continued to skip class, party, sleep late, and fail assignments and tests. I was drinking alcohol, smoking cigarettes, eating terribly... *and having a blast.*

I discovered something very interesting when I was in college regarding all those nights of insomnia I experienced in middle school and high school. During my freshman year at KU, almost every night at 10:30 (except the nights I went out), I would venture off to the vending machines in my dormitory and drink a can of Diet Mountain Dew.

Ironically, this potent caffeinated beverage put me right to sleep!

It is important to mention this small piece of the puzzle since the reason most people don't consume Diet Mountain Dew before bedtime is because caffeine usually keeps people awake. *Not me… in fact, the result was just the opposite.* After drinking the caffeinated drink, I went right to sleep for 6 to 8 hours.

In hindsight, this observation is consistent with signal transduction and neurotransmitter communication in patients with ADHD, and explains why the caffeine/stimulant effect of the caffeine was calming and put me right to sleep. So within 30 to 40 minutes of consuming the potent beverage, I actually felt pretty calm. I remember lying on the top bunk bed of my dorm room and feeling relaxed, listening to some slow jams, then turning the music off and going right to sleep. While I didn't realize **why** this happened, I inadvertently found a way to sleep. This was *ONE* good thing that came out of my time in Lawrence!

Thanks to my newfound freedom, and the fact that no one was really checking in on me, I ended up with a 1.6 GPA for my freshman year.

Thus, summer school was unavoidable. Here we go... *again.* At least this time I had a choice: a community college in St. Louis or the KU Summer Program. I begged my parents to allow me to stay at KU to attend summer school instead of attending the St. Louis Community College they strongly encouraged. With great hesitation, they agreed to allow me to stay in Lawrence... *if* I lived with my studious friends and attended class religiously. They didn't make me get a job because they wanted me to focus on school and improving my grades.

It may come as no surprise, but that decision was an **even** bigger mistake. Not only did I **not** go to class, I didn't care enough to withdraw from the courses I was failing. Now I was at Blutarsky level: I earned a 0.0. And yet, I could not have cared less about school, grades, or pleasing anyone. And worse, I didn't care about making the grades to achieve my goal of becoming a nurse.

That was the end of my KU life.

This was an all-time low for me.

I blew my chance of attending an out of state college — or any college at that point — and justifiably so, my parents did not trust me. I knew I had disappointed them tremendously.

**There was no self-love at this point
and I was really sad. I was quiet,
felt very alone, and became reclusive.**

I was sinking. It was getting harder and harder
to keep treading water — to keep my head
above the surface. I felt like I was drowning and
I couldn't call for help. I needed a lifeboat before
I sank to the bottom.

I needed to be rescued.

"*Everything you've ever wanted is on the other side of fear.*"

— GEORGE ADDAIR

11

Turning Point

My parents brought me back to St. Louis to live with them, as it was obvious that my way was **clearly** not working.

I lived in their house under their rules. I had a 10 p.m. curfew and **NO** going out on weeknights. Although I was over 18, and legally did not have to agree, I had no other options.

I had no money, had flunked out of college, had very few friends, and was depressed. I complied with my parents' demands, which included structure, schedules, and rules.

I worked two part-time jobs and attended classes at the local community college.

The money I made working as a hostess at a restaurant and at a tanning salon went directly to my dad. Every paycheck received was immediately signed over to him. It was a clear expectation that I was to pay back the money he spent on my tuition — the money I threw away while at KU.

This was one of the best lessons I had ever learned, and a big turning point in my life.

We were fortunate to grow up in an environment with caring parents who worked hard to support us. My parents were financially stable — they didn't need me to pay them back for the blown year at KU. That was not their point. They were teaching me the value of hard work. They were teaching me that I threw away what could have been a great opportunity at KU.

Furthermore, they wanted me to see first-hand how hard one has to work to make money. Once I realized how much money, time, and trust was utterly wasted, they knew that I would strive to be the best person I could be. I wanted to pay them back for the tuition that I flushed down the toilet.

I wanted to help myself accomplish my dream of becoming a nurse. And, I wanted to earn their trust again.

My mom and dad knew I could do it. They believed in me at a time when I didn't believe in myself.

I remember the day they looked at me when I was at the community college and said, "We believe in you and we know you can do it, but *you* need to believe you can do it. You need to *give* yourself a real chance."

My parents were confident that my impulsive and irresponsible behavior exhibited at KU was related to something deeper – some kind of underlying medical condition or learning disability.

As a result of their suspicions, when I was 19 years old, they contacted a team of physicians to perform a thorough medical and psychological evaluation.

My parents consulted nationally recognized pediatric and adolescent neurologist, Dr. Garrett Burris. They also consulted a psychologist, my pediatrician, and a speech therapist. They were all to meet me and evaluate me independently, then collaborate and discuss their findings.

Good grief, something good *HAD* to come from this meeting! They discussed and reviewed the previous records from the PhD/Education Specialist back in 1985, all my previous therapy consultations, and my academic records.

After several multidisciplinary
meetings and thorough physical
and psychological evaluations,
the unanimous and conclusive
diagnosis of ADHD* was made in 1992.

I was relieved to finally hear there was a reason for the fog. The diagnosis gave me the "why." It explained the feeling of swimming frantically and getting nowhere. The feeling of sinking below the surface and struggling to keep from drowning... Now I needed to figure out the "how."

---

* See chapters 17 and 18 for ADHD information, data and statistics.

"Life begins
at the end
of your comfort zone."

— **ANONYMOUS**

12

The Mask

Many people find comfort hiding insecurities and fears by "putting on a front" for the outside world.

It is easier to project a happy, funny, confident exterior than reveal the reality of painful internal struggles that exist.

Everyone has insecurities. ***NO ONE breezes through life.*** If we don't struggle to overcome obstacles, we can never truly appreciate the sweet satisfaction that comes with success.

The façade is inevitable for a lot of people and is a result of the society in which we live.

Many people are too vain or too proud to admit they need help. Some feel the need to appear perfect, even though they may actually be falling apart. The truth is, we are all imperfect.

We all think everyone else has it so easy, or that others do not struggle — *BUT THEY DO!*

As I have gotten older and wiser, I have learned a valuable lesson: it is much easier to be honest with myself and others than to put on a front. Keeping up a façade can be exhausting.

You are acting... pretending that everything is great on the outside while covering up the truth. Then, when you are alone in your sanctuary — be it your bedroom, dorm room, or anywhere you are unafraid to be afraid — the real fears come to fruition. Not only are you dealing with the reality of actual insecurities and struggles, but you must also bear the mental and physical strain from upholding the farce for so long.

I have learned that authenticity and honesty are essential in life. Be gentle with yourself and know that **NO ONE is perfect**. No one makes it through life free from any battle wounds. The more candid I am, the more self-deprecating and genuine, the better. The result: inner peace and happiness. Chances are that what you are worrying about, dreading, or feeling insecure about, are the same things many others experience.

This realization was a vital part of my journey because it was important to recognize that I was not alone in facing my struggles throughout life. No matter what, it is important to always be real, be authentic, and throw away the mask; face the reality of who you are and what you are going through.

Throwing away the mask doesn't mean advertising personal issues and obstacles, but it does allow one to be free of a façade. It is liberating to let go of the societal-imposed need for perfection and embrace all of who you really are — the good *and* the not so good qualities.

It took me a LONG time to realize that my ADHD was one of the best parts of me.

It is why I am the successful mother, wife, friend, nurse, daughter, and sister that I am today.

Once I took an account of my life, I worked to rectify some of the wrongs I had committed, including making amends with my close high-school friend whom I hurt when I disinvited him to my graduation dance. Recently, I shared with him this book, and my desire to help others who may be living trapped with ADHD. He was shocked to hear the real story. He had no idea I ever felt trapped — or felt like I was drowning — while growing up with undiagnosed ADHD.

After reading my story, my friend remarked, "I'm stunned! *NO WAY!! YOU* were depressed in high school? *YOU!?*"

I explained how depressed, unhappy, and insecure I felt throughout high school. He was dumbfounded. He had always thought of me as a confident, spontaneous girl with positive energy and an infectious laugh.

Now *I* was the one who was stunned. I could not believe that was the impression I had projected. The "me" that others viewed from the outside wasn't the "me" I truly was on the inside. We discussed openly the trials and struggles I had faced and overcome to become the successful woman I am today. He said, "Your positive exterior protected your insecure interior."

Smart man, my friend!

"Believe you can and you're halfway there."

— THEODORE ROOSEVELT

13

Becoming Florence

Once the official diagnosis of ADHD was made,
and we were certain that I possessed the "text
book" symptoms of a 19-year-old female with
"ADHD Hyperactive type." The neurologist
prescribed Ritalin SR 20 mg, twice a day.

And everything changed...

CLEAR, FOCUSED, CALM, and IN CONTROL
are the words I can use to best describe how
I felt once I took the medication as prescribed.

The "snow" vanished from the TV screen...

The windshield wipers cleared the glass...

THE FOG LIFTED!

When I was drowning, my parents were the boat
that rescued me — pulling me towards shore. The
ongoing consultation and unwavering support of
Dr. Burris was a 'lifeline' that subsequently gave
me the mental stamina and physical strength to

leave the comfort and safety of that boat and swim on my own.

To this day, it's still almost impossible to fathom how crystal clear my world became within hours of taking the right medication.

My thoughts were clear and concise.

My brain was 'working.'

Finding the correct medication is a lifesaver for people suffering from ADHD (refractory to non-pharmacological methods). In my case, years of therapy and trials of *NINE* non-drug methods brought no relief. In my case, I would need a medicinal intervention to help my brain get into an unfamiliar but desperately needed symbiosis.

Because ADHD is a neurochemical condition involving neurotransmitter communication, pharmacological treatment (in many cases) is necessary. Let me be clear: Diet, sleep, exercise, and a regimented schedule are essential for success. Medication should be a LAST resort, not a first step.

Determining which medication provides the best symptom relief can be difficult, and can require some trial and error before the most effective choice is found. *(http://psychiatric-disorders.com/adhd/adhd-medication-treatments/2014/)*

I find it fascinating as a heart and vascular clinical expert, and a classic ADHD patient, to experience the phenomenon of taking a 'stimulant' to 'calm' the brain.

My pharmacological knowledge as an advanced practice nurse assisted my understanding of how stimulant medications 'work' to calm the brain in patients with ADHD. The neurotransmitter response with enhanced synapse communication is an extraordinary breakthrough in treating the symptoms of patients with ADHD.

While I felt the immediate impact of my new reality, it would take some work to convince others. Regardless of my newfound clarity and focus, my parents continued to keep a tight leash on me. They were concerned about my past history and the partying that occurred at KU. They were even more inclined to monitor me while taking this Schedule II medication, Ritalin.

I still had to comply with their strict curfew. I maintained a low sugar diet, regimented sleep schedule, and limited alcohol consumption. On the surface, it might sound like rules for a prisoner; to me, it was just the opposite.

I loved the routine and structure.

At 20 years old, being happy spending the evening studying, rather than going out to bars with friends, was a far cry from what made me happy the year before at KU. It felt good to be clear-minded, balanced, and productive.

This once careless, inattentive, hyperactive, **unfocused** girl, now had a part-time job working at a restaurant to earn money to pay my dad back for the tuition he wasted at KU. I continued to volunteer both at the nursing home (as I had for years) and at a battered women's shelter during the time I was living at my parent's house. I was **focused** and determined to pay my parents back, and to get excellent grades at the community college. Not only was I focused... I was **hyperfocused**.

> According to Pepperdine University, some people with ADHD may become hyperfocused. This makes them so intently focused on a task that they may not even notice the world around them. The benefit to this is when given an assignment, a person with ADHD may work at it until its' completion without breaking concentration.

I was on track. I felt great. I had self-love.

After 6 months of complying with the rules at my parents' house and maintaining a 4.0 GPA at the community college, my parents said they would give me a second chance and support me if I was accepted to one specific nursing school, Valparaiso University. I could not believe it. I was so happy that they would provide another opportunity for me to achieve my dream to become a nurse ... especially after providing such past disappointment.

Their condition was that I needed to continue on my new positive path through May... equalling one full year. The positive path included structure, routine, medication, and continued good grades. If I stayed on course and was accepted to VU College of Nursing, I would be able to attend.

Well, I am proud to say that I was accepted to the college of nursing! I was accepted like other candidates, fair and square, with no academic conditions. That feeling was amazing — maybe as good as the feeling of graduating high school... maybe even better.

My parents and I made another pact. They would support my journey at VU *if*: I lived on campus in the dorm, had a bike — not a car — to get to and from class, and promised there would be no partying. I complied, and was thrilled to start the greatest journey of my life.

I loved the smaller size of the private college versus the much larger KU. I also loved my structured little dorm room. I had the surprising good fortune of not having a roommate (that was a great move by the way). I didn't have a car to tempt me to go out, and I was ready to do everything necessary to start living my dream.

It was easy to agree to the terms. It was also easy to focus on my classes, as my mind was clear now. I LOVED the feeling of being clear-minded, focused, and diligent during this time in my life. I admit that it was not the medication alone that facilitated my success; it was the combination of proper diet, ample sleep, less partying, *and* taking my medication as prescribed that allowed me to be the person I had always wanted to be, but had doubted would ever be possible.

I remember my dad riding the aqua colored Schwinn bicycle back to my dormitory from the local Wal-Mart one day, while I followed behind driving his car. I still laugh out loud when I reminisce about that beautiful, sunny, summer day that he rode it down Highway 30 back to my dorm, while I was driving his fancy car. He was determined that I would have everything I needed during my time at VU. Since the bike was too big to fit in his fancy sports car, *he* rode it back to my dorm. He looked hilarious on the teal colored woman's bike, pedaling down the shoulder of a four-lane highway. I always get a kick out of my dad. I hope that one day when I'm old and gray the visual of that moment never abandons me.

Before he left to go back to St. Louis, he looked at me and said, "I know you will make yourself, your mother, and me very proud. You **CAN** do this. We believe in you, and now we know you finally believe in yourself. That is all you need to be successful. You can do this."

I went to class religiously. Every day, I would arrive to class early so I could get a seat in the first two rows of the auditorium. Surprisingly, I moved to a different seat away from disruptive or chatty students. I transcribed my notes long-hand, and then, after class, I would review my notes and type them out neatly on a computer in the shared dorm computer lab. This was a method that worked for me in two ways:

1. Transcribing longhand kept me focused during class and engaged in what the professor was saying.
2. While typing the notes later, I was able to remediate the information. The repetition was

beneficial in memorizing and learning new concepts. Typing the notes also helped me identify concepts that I did not understand.

Organization, time management, and self-discipline were key tools I implemented, and the outcome was good grades.

I absolutely loved nursing school. This was my dream becoming a reality. I loved wearing all white to clinicals in the various community hospitals. I loved getting up early, driving in car pools with other nursing students to the various clinical settings, and could not contain my excitement and sheer joy! I was accepted and loved by my nursing peers, and I shared so much in common with them. I felt a sense of belonging to a group, of fitting in, while at the same time being able to focus on all of the tasks at hand. I found value and self-worth when caring for others. The end of my awakening was within reach.

I can never thank my parents enough for their support and guidance. They gave me a conservative financial allowance for necessities. Without unlimited funds to tempt me, I kept myself on a pretty tight schedule. The medication, along with healthy habits, kept me on track. I felt awesome! It is amazing what their correspondence did for my self-esteem.

My whole family sent encouraging cards and packages — writing about how proud they were of my hard work and commitment. I found the cards recently, and reading them brought back the positive feelings I experienced all those years ago. The support of my family was constant and definitely contributed to my solid academic performance. Before I knew it, I was maintaining a 3.3 GPA in a top nursing school. In my wildest imaginings, I never thought I was capable of pulling it off.

I liked the quaint dorm room as my residence at school; I liked riding my bike to get around campus; and I really liked the small college of nursing and faith-based education I was receiving at VU. Things were on a roll, and I felt in control of my life.

I made wonderful friends in nursing school who shared my same drive and determination. I continued to exercise. I was in a stable and happy emotional place. I did not have any tutors or therapists at VU — this was a first for me — and it was a thrill to be able to stand on my own without fear... to know that I was responsible for my actions, and to be able to trust myself with my decision making.

I still maintained visits with my St. Louis physicians, and provided monthly feedback to Dr. Burris, as he was prescribing the Ritalin.

While the implementation of Ritalin was a godsend in my life, I should take this opportunity to warn you. One note of caution is that when taking a Schedule II medication, such as Ritalin, one must be aware of the adverse effects while taking this class of medication. Ritalin, and other stimulants, can increase the 'drive' or desire to crave nicotine, caffeine, and alcohol. There is a slight physiological connection between taking a stimulant, such as Ritalin, and an increase in caffeine or alcohol consumption.

However, recent Research from *ADDA.org* shows that "those patients with properly physician diagnosed ADHD who are treated with correct medication have a 23% less incidence of abusing illicit street drugs and/or alcohol." The belief among expert physicians is that young adults often self-medicate with street drugs and alcohol to 'calm' their brain activity and distraction.

Recent findings of ADHD medication and the risk of future substance abuse, noted in the Journal of the American Medical Association (JAMA) Psychiatry, were based on a meta-analysis of 15 previous studies, from 1980 to 2012, that included more than 2,500 participants with ADHD, some of whom were pre-scribed medication and some of whom were not. Results demonstrated that there was no association between the use of stimulant medication and future abuse of alcohol or illicit substances.

Researchers at the University of California reported finding "no association between the use of medica-tion such as Ritalin and future abuse of alcohol, nicotine, marijuana and cocaine," *(according to lead author Kathryn Humphreys, a doctoral candidate in UCLA's department of psychology).*

As a result, researchers said their work provides "an important update" to the body of knowledge about drug abuse and ADHD medications." *(JAMA, 2013.)*

And just when I thought I had everything planned out for the rest of my life, fate threw me a curve. On September 24, 1993, while attending VU College of Nursing, the most incredible thing happened to me that forever changed my life for the better. I met my future husband, Jim.

He graduated from the University of Notre Dame three years prior, and was working as a futures and commodities trader in Chicago. Jim was at Valparaiso University visiting his younger brother when we met at a party. I immediately fell for him... hook, line, and sinker.

I adored Jim and Jim adored me — wit, humor, impulsivity, and all. Jim knew when I had to study, and supported my structured routine. Seriously, it had to be karma, or fate, or a blind squirrel finding an acorn. What incredible timing — to meet Jim during one of his few visits to see his brother when he lived in a different state, especially since I never attended fraternity parties.

Well... at least not since turning over a new leaf!

He is, and always has been, my biggest fan and supporter since the day we met. I love him so much. Throughout nursing school, he helped me with papers and projects, and even helped me type my class notes.

The stars had finally aligned. I had my profession. I had my man.

I finally felt a true sense of balance for the first time in my life.

Sadly, that euphoria would be short lived. As Charles Dickens wrote, "It was the best of times, it was the worst of times..." And, that's how it was for me, shortly after meeting Jim.

I endured one of the most difficult times of my life during the winter of 1994. I lost my best friend and dorm mate, Laura. She was killed instantly in a terrible car accident while driving home from nursing clinical (in the middle of the day) on February 24, 1994. It was incredibly difficult to lose a 22-year-old, beautiful, loving, sister-type of friend who adored me as much as I adored her. Devastated will never come close to describing how soul-crushing it truly was.

Together, Jim and I worked through the process of grieving. I started to see a counselor who helped me work through my grief and pain. He assisted me in resuming a somewhat new normal life at school. Jim provided comfort and helped me heal as well. Together we planted a tree to symbolize new life and to always remember Laura on the grounds of the nursing school. Jim and his brother were there for the dedication. We worked to raise money for a memorial in Laura's honor at VU. The tree and plaque still stand today.

She would always say, "You're not hyper! You are unique, and I love you!" I always smile when I think of Laura and her description of me.

I persevered through the Bachelor of Science in Nursing program at VU and graduated with a

3.0 GPA and my BSN Degree on May 21, 1995. Easily, one of the proudest days of my life!

I did it! I got my nursing degree from a respected nursing school, essentially on time... within four years and one summer!!!

I DID IT!

This was an even bigger accomplishment since I had blown off the entire first year at KU. To start over, pull it together, attend class year round, and attend clinical was no easy task.

I could not be more proud of myself and my dedication and hard work spent in achieving my goal.

I am eternally grateful to my parents for giving me every chance and opportunity to succeed. There is no way I would be where I am today if they hadn't given me a second chance to attend an ideal nursing school. I also never would have met my soul-mate, Jim. I am proud to share that Jim and I just celebrated 19 years of marriage. That is quite a milestone for most couples; however, it is even more unusual to find such longevity in couples with an ADHD spouse. Jim has eternal patience and unconditional love, and we work to maintain open and honest communication... always.

Following completion of my BSN, I continued on Ritalin after graduation so I could focus well enough to take NCLEX-RN National Certification Licensure Exam for Registered Nurses. I knew that it would be a long and challenging standardized exam. Dr. Burris and I discussed my options for taking the test, and he encouraged me to maintain the status quo: remain on the medication until successful completion of RN boards. After the boards, we would re-evaluate whether or not to continue the medication.

I studied full-time for boards during the summer of 1995. When I set my mind to something, I do go all the way. I took studying for boards to a whole new level — including commuting by train to the closest Kaplan center in downtown Chicago. I studied and reviewed all day, every day, five days a week. I took practice exams via the computer (the NCLEX-RN boards went live with computerized testing the summer of 1995, it was the first time the test was not administered as a written exam), and did everything possible to help myself pass the test. Following two months of autonomous, self-directed review and practice tests, I felt ready to go in and kill it. I prayed the night before the exam for a calm, clear mind. I knew the material backwards and forwards, inside and out. What I did not know was if my anxiety or self-induced pressure would prevent me from being successful. In my heart, I knew I did everything recommended — and more so — to prepare for the NCLEX-RN exam.

On August 22, 1995, I took the computerized timed test in a testing center, just like everyone else. I was legally permitted to take the test untimed because of the ADHD diagnosis, as I had a letter from Dr. Burris. To no one's surprise, I insisted on taking the board exam like everyone else. The next month, I got my results. I aced them… 75/75 questions! I could not believe it!! I thought I failed the test. I thought it was a long and difficult exam, and was not so sure I passed when the screen shut down. Then I had to wait two weeks for the results. That was agony for me. As I have stated throughout this journey, I am not a patient person. It was the longest two weeks that I can remember, each passing day feeling like a week. Finally, when the results came via the mail, my anticipation was on overload.

"Congratulations, Mary Kristin, RN, you passed the NCLEX-RN state board certification exam." I was ecstatic as I read the letter! I remember my

eyes filling up with tears of joy. I was so elated.
I did it — I became a registered nurse — because
I did not quit, and because I worked hard.

That was the most memorable and pivotal
professional moment in my life. I felt confident
and fulfilled. I was at the top of my game; I
passed RN boards, was dating a great guy, living
independently, and was ready to finally work as a
staff RN. I contacted Dr. Burris to share that I had
successfully passed boards, and he was delighted
to hear of my achievement. He and I discussed
the importance of everything working together:
the medication, a healthy diet low in sugar and
caffeine, ample sleep, maintaining regular doctor
appointments, and most of all, my hard work
in school and determination that led to my victory
of passing boards.

We agreed it would be best to see if I got a
staff nursing job, and how I would acclimate to
shift work, before we made a plan to wean off the
medication.

There was an abundance of nurses applying
for jobs. So, as a new graduate it was difficult to
find a job as a nurse in a hospital setting.

Nevertheless, in September, 1995, I received a
staff nurse position at a small community hospital
in Hobart, Indiana. I worked full-time on a

telemetry unit. Jim and I remained dating in a committed relationship, and our love for each other was undeniable. I loved my job working as a floor nurse on a cardiology unit. I enjoyed comforting others during a time of need or illness. It brought me such satisfaction hearing, "Will you please be my nurse tomorrow, too?" or, "What time do you go home?" The veteran, more experienced nurses always told me during training that when patients ask you what time your shift is over, it means they like you.

When I put my scrubs on each day before heading into work, I felt smart and I felt happy. I felt that I was working a noble job in an honorable profession. I thought to myself, *'This must be what success feels like.'*

Working shift work as a floor nurse is certainly a tough job physically as well as mentally; but I loved it, and I was good at it... we thrive when we do things we love, resulting in self-love.

In November of 1995, I weaned off the Ritalin per my physician's order and continued to work shift work on the cardiac monitoring unit. I felt essentially the same, but a little more 'quick' to do things, sometimes without considering the consequences.

In other words, I was not thinking things

through. I was moving right along a little more careless and scattered. In fact, I made a medication error at work because I was stressed about getting the 0900 medications passed out on time, and administered insulin to a non-diabetic patient. We figured it out right away, gave the patient orange juice, and she was okay... *thank God!* However, I had to complete an incident report, tell the patient what happened, and talk to the unit manager about the error. I also had to slow down.

I have no doubt the medication error was the result of many things, not solely the result of being off the Ritalin. I found that concentrating on deep breathing and carefully reviewing the Five Rights of Medication Administration before giving medication to a patient was helpful. However, sadly, that old familiar feeling had crept into my life again.

The fog was back.

I also found that I was slacking with regard to the responsibilities of my apartment. One instance I remember was that I forgot to pay my NIPSCO gas bill. Thankfully, the gas was not turned off. When I received a 'disconnect gas warning' via the mail, I paid the bill immediately. The forgetfulness and carelessness were things I had not experienced in a long time.

I overslept for a few shifts of work, was scattered with tasks and documentation at work, and was rarely able to leave work when my shift ended. Unproductive and unfocused, I telephoned Dr. Burris around January, 1996, six months after stopping the medication.

He requested a face-to-face meeting in his office. Such a visit provides Dr. Burris with clearer data that he may not obtain via virtual contact. It is a more thorough evaluation, and the recent regression warranted more than a quick update.

We agreed it was best to resume the Ritalin 20mg twice a day on work days and only once daily on off days. As we knew from past experience, the medicine helped me with focus and task completion. There was no doubt in either of our minds that I was more focused, less hyper-sensitive, more productive, and more settled while on the medication.

In August of 1997, I decided to pursue my Master's Degree while still working full-time as a staff nurse. I thought, *'Why not pursue this advanced degree as it will offer me more flexibility later in life?'*

At this point, Jim and I were engaged and

I was working full-time at St. Mary's Hospital on a Cardiology Unit. I applied to Purdue University Calumet School of Nursing for the Master of Science Degree. I was thrilled to be accepted to the program as it was highly reputable, and the commutable distance allowed me to work part-time while attending school full-time.

Diligence and dedication were the tools I used to get where I wanted to go.

In fact, I graduated with a 3.7 GPA on a 4.0 scale.

Sometimes when things go right, it's important to take an inventory of why they're going right. I was working my dream job while continuing my education, now married to my best friend and soul mate. I had loving and supportive family and friends and was fortunate to be so cared about during my journey.

I had even received a financial grant covering 50% of the cost of my master's degree program as a result of my undergraduate GPA! I'm living proof: it pays to stay in school!

While attending graduate school at Purdue University-Calumet, I was focused on being successful in all areas including classwork and clinical training. If you throw in an opportunity to work at the University of Chicago in the Cardiac Care Unit for my Master's degree, my life had reached a state of nirvana. Amazing things were happening as a result of hard work, dedication, discipline, and yes, medication.

I was one of the only graduate nursing students who drove one hour each way to the University of Chicago Hospital, in Hyde Park, to do my critical care clinical experience. I was eager to learn as much as possible in my pathophysiology class. My favorite unit was Congestive Heart Failure. I was especially intrigued by heart transplantation and mechanical circulatory support (TAH, VADs and ECMO) during clinical training. I loved my preceptor, Melinda, who was a Cardiology Clinical Nurse Specialist.

I learned a tremendous amount from Melinda. I looked up to her and thought of her as a great role model. She embodied all the skills of an exemplary advanced practice nurse: being able to multi-task, being a patient advocate and being a clinical resource for fellow clinicians.

Training at U of C during graduate school definitely sparked my interest and drove my desire to specialize in Cardiac Critical Care Nursing. I was passionate about everything in Cardiology — the pathophysiology of various cardiac conditions,

the patients, and the cutting edge therapies
and treatments.

I was so hyper-focused while learning about
heart transplantation that I asked the nurses who
knew me from training to call me when one of the
CHF patients was to be transplanted — this could
be on any day, and at any hour.

One of the CCU RNs called me in middle of
the night, woke me, and informed me that a heart
was en route. One of our patients was going to
be a transplanted in the next few hours and if
I wanted to observe, I should come ASAP. (Keep
in mind, I lived in Northwest Indiana, about an
hour from the hospital.)

I did not care that I was driving back to U of C
in middle of the night — exhausted and excited at
the same time — I wanted to witness this incredible
operation that would change a young patient's
life forever. It was an amazing experience and
unforgettable to observe that transplant surgery.
I remember thinking to myself, *'I really LOVE what
I am learning. I want to be a Clinical Nurse Specialist
in Cardiology, subspecializing in Congestive Heart
Failure.'* My experience at U of C, combined with
my outstanding Pathophysiology Professor at
Purdue, fueled my passion and stamina to learn
as much as possible about cardiovascular nursing.

Many of my classmates in graduate school performed their clinical experiences where they were already employed, or a local clinic or hospital. Not me. I was enthralled and hyper-focused. I had to be at *the best* hospital with *the best* preceptor, and asserted myself in cool clinical situations to learn as much as possible.

I felt a sense of pride in training with world class Cardiologists at U of C. I loved that no one at U of C knew of my unsuccessful past. I loved that they did not know the struggles I overcame to now be training alongside them at a top cardiac center. I loved my brilliant preceptor and loved being a part of a healthcare team. I knew then that I wanted to work at a large teaching hospital in cardiology for my nursing career.

As productive and busy as my life was, I experienced occasional anxiety. Considering the busy work schedule along with attending graduate school, being newly married, and working clinical hours, I was understandably anxious. Knowing the positive effect endorphins have on the mind via exercise, I made time for daily power walks. I discovered walking briskly significantly reduced the angst I was feeling, and I made sure I made time for exercise.

My focus was enhanced while working the

plan of getting exercise and sleep, not abusing alcohol, and taking Ritalin. I paid attention in class, took solid notes, and knew when I needed to take a break or move around. I was self-aware, productive, and successful at home, at school, and at work.

Speaking of work, just a side note about taking a schedule II medication and employment: ***It is critical to communicate all medications you are taking, including over the counter, and the reasons they are prescribed, to your employer.*** A pediatrician, neurologist, psychologist or psychiatrist — whoever is prescribing a scheduled II medication — must provide accurate and current documentation as to why the scheduled II medication is being prescribed. One of the many reasons for this information to be shared with an employer is because when a routine, pre-employment drug screen is performed, human resources will have adequate physician explanation if there is question about the results consistent with Ritalin. To clarify, many people with ADHD who are treated with medication are not on doses high enough to cause any significant peak in blood or urine screens, but full disclosure is essential in the workplace.

Academically, professionally, and personally, my life had come back into balance. I was happy. I was on time for shifts. I communicated clear and concise patient reports to the following shift nurse without forgetting key information.

My impulsivity was kept in check; I was not spending money frivolously, or snapping at my new husband out of frustration from other stressors.

I was in control of my life, and my behavior, and it felt good.

Life continued on this path through the completion of my Master of Science Degree (3.7 GPA). At this point, I also had four years of experience as a staff nurse under my belt.

The next two years flew by. I had six years of inpatient clinical nurse experience and was eager to work as a Clinical Nurse Specialist in a large metropolitan teaching facility.

In June of 2000, Jim and I moved back to my hometown of St. Louis as we landed great jobs — and had friends and family waiting in the wings.

Now it was time to wean off the Ritalin. The summer we moved back to St. Louis, I met with Dr. Burris and we agreed that upon successful completion of the Clinical Nurse Specialist licensing exam, it would be a good idea to discontinue the Ritalin. An important factor in this decision was the desire to have children. Women of childbearing age who want to have children should be off stimulant medication well in advance of becoming pregnant.

Moving forward with discontinuing the Ritalin was not a problem. Fortunately, my husband, extended family, friends, doctors, and employer did not notice any mal effects as a result of discontinuing the medication. Professionally, personally, and financially, we were unaffected by my stopping the medication. Stability, consistency, and routine are essential in maintaining success in all facets of life for people with ADHD. It is paramount for you to be aware of what to expect regarding possible physical and mental repercussions from discontinuing medication.

Maintaining structure, organization, routine, ample sleep, and a proper diet low in caffeine and sugars are only some of the things I must do to maintain my life with ADHD. I have been extremely successful on and off medication. I am confident that correct medication can enable those living with ADHD to experience what 'calm brain' feels like and then learn how to maintain that feeling. I am very self-aware about what I need to do to maintain a successful, healthy, happy life.

ADHD is one of the reasons I am successful. I can multi-task, I can hyper-focus, I can be energetic and have fun with my friends, and I can be an attentive mother to our children.

Without a doubt, the *MOST* important and significant aspects of success with ADHD include the following: A supportive and understanding home environment, especially with concerned and involved parents, a medical expert, and involvement of the child's teachers and coaches who collaborate on a realistic treatment plan. Ideally, the experts should partner with the child's pediatrician and parents.

The medical, educational, and parental support system, working together, will directly affect the outcomes and successes for the child. I know first-hand the importance and effectiveness of a fully-committed team. Medication, in addition to the support team, can impact a child's academic, social, and personal outcomes drastically.

A holistic approach lends itself to globally positive outcomes.

My determination and tenacity, along with the love and support demonstrated by my parents and husband, were essential in my success.

I have ADHD. I am confident that overcoming obstacles and dealing with ADHD contributed to my success in life — just as much as it contributed to my challenges.

I had frequent visits with Dr. Burris, especially during the initial stages of medication management. These visits were important as they included face-to-face discussions that provided him the subjective and objective patient data necessary to continue the plan of care. Dr. Burris was always approachable. I could ask him anything. He never made me feel embarrassed or stupid. He made sure I had regularly scheduled appointments, necessary in monitoring positive or negative outcomes with use of a scheduled medication such as Ritalin. Dr. Burris was supportive, empathetic, responsive, patient, and *always* willing to listen.

*"Ask, and
you shall receive.
Search and
you will find.
Knock and
the door will be
opened to you."*

— **MATTHEW 7:7**

14

Happily Ever After

The effects of ADHD on a marriage are many, for both the ADHD spouse, and the non-ADHD spouse.

If both spouses suffer from ADHD, the impact can be devastating. Research shows that misunderstandings and challenges associated with ADHD can significantly hamper successful marriages. The statistics on ADHD marriages are not promising. An individual diagnosed with ADHD is *TWICE* as likely to be divorced as one who does not have ADHD.

> **Approximately 60% of relationships with at least one partner with ADHD are significantly dysfunctional, which is twice the percent of non-ADHD relationships.**

A multifaceted and multiple-step approach is shown to be helpful. Understanding how ADHD affects your marriage is key. Developing empathy and forgiveness for your ADHD spouse is a great first step toward building a successful marriage.

Keys to Building and Maintaining a Healthy Marriage:

✔ Seeking and accepting appropriate treatment for the ADHD and non-ADHD spouse.

✔ Developing positive, safe, and collaborative communication habits.

✔ Setting appropriate personal boundaries.

✔ Reconnecting and rebuilding the romance.

All of these steps are aimed at improving the resilience of the ADHD marriage. My husband and I have been happily married for 18 years. He is my best friend, my confidant, and biggest fan. My husband has the patience of a saint, humor that is spot-on, and genuine kindness that never ceases to amaze me. I am not an easy person to live with... ***but I am FUN!***

On a more serious note, Jim and I have learned over the years that open and honest communication is essential to our successful marriage. We laugh, yell, cry, pray, and talk about everything.

Jim and I put our marriage first and consistently make time for one another. We always think about each other's feelings and how our actions or words may affect the other before we do or say something. We argue, fight, and get mad just like everyone else, but we manage to make-up and learn from each situation.

One example of how we put our relationship first is that we 'play hooky' from work and the kids to have time alone in our house together. We genuinely enjoy each other's company. We decided that taking a day every few months to meet for lunch, sit on our porch, go to a movie, or shop for kids' birthday gifts was a great tool for our relationship. It is an important aspect of our communication as we are not interrupted by our children, work calls, or the craziness of life.

Last October, we drove our girls to school together, dropped them off, then headed back home. We talked over coffee at the kitchen table, took a walk, and chatted over lunch outside at Cafe Napoli. We enjoyed the clear, glorious, crisp, fall day as we sipped on Prosecco and reminisced for two hours. When the waiter asked how long we had been married, we replied, "18 years." He said it was nice to see a married couple enjoying each other after that many years together. It was a great day!

When one of us is having a bad day and the other feels as though they can't win or say anything right, we take 'time out.' We go to other rooms in our house and take an hour or two away from one another — take time to reflect and chill. Often, that's all we need to realize that what we were fighting about is *so* not worth it.

Nursing is the most ideal profession for me as it involves constant movement *and* taking care of people. The unique experience with each patient means there is no monotony. Wearing scrubs is awesome because they are comfortable clothes — and, I look like my peers *(remember the uniform story?)*. I feel important wearing scrubs and calling myself 'nurse.' Many people with ADHD struggle with keeping the same job for a prolonged period of time. Fifteen years later, I am proud to say that I work for the same incredible boss, at the same medical center, in an advanced practice nurse role that requires a high level of responsibility.

The role is ever changing and sometimes brings challenges. I thrive when faced with challenges, and I never quit.

Where there is a will, there is a way.

I am fortunate to have a boss who totally understands me... so much so that she created the Advanced Practice Nurse (APN) role I currently assume which compliments my attributes. She has supported me through many professional triumphs and challenges. I am confident that my professional success is predominantly the result of my incredibly loyal, bright, supportive, and caring boss. Her philosophy for staff to put family first — even before work — results in staff who are more diligent, efficient, and dedicated, and fosters a positive attitude and work environment. She puts employees in roles that 'fit' their unique traits resulting in their being more productive and rewarding.

As part of my role, I travel to local referring hospitals to teach about clinical trials, and novel treatment modalities, while also participating on various committees. I could not love my position, my team, or my boss more than I do. She understands the constant movement and critical thinking are keys to my success. She is a blessing. I am confident that my professional success would not be the same had I not been working for her the past 15 years.

In October 2015, I read an article about a

man who was 50 years old, unemployed, and recently divorced. In the article, he said that he was not hirable or insurable as a result of impulsivity that was never diagnosed — he was certain it was probably ADHD. It was sad to read the article about someone never accurately diagnosed, and how lost he was so late in life.

I am hopeful that people realize and understand that ADHD can be an asset and a benefit in life, not just a detriment.

It takes hard work, dedication, and faith to live successfully and happily with ADHD. One must be committed to working the program, and have proper and adequate support in order to be successful. Then again, this is true with almost everything in life.

> The MTA study, the multi-modal treatment assessment study, the largest study ever done on the treatment of ADHD in children, provides a wealth of knowledge. It is remarkable because the subjects in the study have been followed for 8 years. The study shows that positive connections with people, especially within the family, make a crucial difference in outcome. The study concluded that while medication makes the biggest difference immediately, as

time goes by other factors come significantly into play, including the skill and knowledge of the doctor providing treatment, as well as the positivity of the connections in the life of the individual. It is time for us all to take the force of connection in life far more seriously than we ever have. *(http://www. drhallowell.com/add-adhd/add-adhd-treatment/)*

It is uncommon for individuals with severe ADHD to have healthy long-term marriages, friendships, and professional relationships, and for this alone, I am blessed. My husband, our 19-year marriage, and our daughters, are of what I am most proud.

It is wonderful to feel confident and fulfilled, but more than anything else, it's wonderful to have self-love.

"The only person you are destined to become is the person you decide to be."

— RALPH W. EMERSON

15

In Mom & Dad's Words

Growing up, Kristin was a handful. The qualities that have made her so successful today, were the very ones that made her difficult to raise.

There are a number of stories... but one of the ones that puts it into perspective follows.

When Kristin was about 15 or 16, she had a curfew like all our children did. This was long before cell phones, and her curfew was 10 p.m.

We had a fairly large home at the time. Our home phone would ring, say around 9:45 p.m., and before we could get it, she would be on the line, "I got it. I got it," hollering at us. We would hang up and think all was ok in river city.

Not. Kristin was placing the call from outside the house, from wherever it happened to be, where she wasn't suppose to be. It was six to nine months before we figured it out.

We could fill pages of stories that would

illustrate her ingenuity — and illustrate her potential if these qualities could be harnessed for constructive things. This was ultimately accomplished with a great deal of work from Kristin and with the support she has addressed in this book. Her impulsivity as a result of her ADD, caused her to be fiercely passionate when she did choose an activity, a friend, or a goal. She was always "in it to win it."

We encouraged her to follow her early instinct to help people. We encouraged her to go ahead and pursue a nursing career, which she seemed to be driven toward.

With increased maturity and drive came increased discipline. She excelled in a four year nursing program and aced her boards on the first try. She went on to receive a Masters in Nursing and currently holds a big job at a large metropolitan hospital.

Her purpose and intensity have allowed her to secure lasting friendships, and a steadfast effort to support her daughters in their academics and activities. With these accomplishments she has gained self-confidence and self-love.

She has made us extremely proud for all she has accomplished.

— *Love, Mom and Dad*

"*Successful people
do what
unsuccessful people
are not willing to do.
Don't wish
it were easier;
wish you were better.*"

— JIM ROHN

16

If the Fog Returns

As an ADHD patient, the mother of an ADHD child, a wife, and as a clinician, I know first hand the ongoing work, discipline, and consistency needed for success with and without medication.

It is time consuming, frustrating and exhausting finding the right medication, adhering to a strict schedule, finding the best tutor/support, following the correct diet, and getting the ideal amount of sleep needed to ensure a well-adjusted, happy child. I truly understand how overwhelming it can be trying to find the optimal treatment plan for your child and how disheartening it can be when the plan isn't working.

ADHD not only affects the person diagnosed with the condition, but also affects the whole family. Siblings get annoyed by the ADHD affected child's behavior, outbursts and needs. Mom is exhausted; Dad is irritated that nothing seems to be working; and sadly, the diagnosed child feels like a failure. ***This condition can be your child's biggest asset, if managed properly.*** Parents need to be gentle with themselves and with all members of the family. It is not easy, but it is worth the effort to witness the evolution of a more confident, secure, happier child.

Some say that being on medication for 6 years, then managing work-life balance successfully off medication for 8 years, is a great accomplishment. It is! However, the need to resume medication in the future is a possiblility — it's OK.

Medication may be discontinued for several reasons including the patient losing weight, experiencing psychosis, or insomnia. Medication can also be discontinued because the patient has matured and developed the appropriate tools and the self-discipline necessary to manage their ADHD symptoms without medicine. They don't "grow out of it" or "get ADHD later in life." People are born with ADHD.

The good news is that ADHD can be managed successfully with ***and*** without medication. People need to acquire tools and develop strategies — such as organization, reminders, post-it-notes, adequate sleep, and proper diet — to perform activities of daily living successfully.

Medications are a crutch for any mental health condition or situational stressor. When you break a limb, you receive a cast and crutches to assist with ambulation while the bone is healing, right? Our bodies need time and therapeutic interventions to heal. Most everyone needs help to get through certain situations, be it actual crutches, splints, talk therapy, medication or counseling. Whatever it is, get the support you need. No plan is a one size fits all and no plan will be unchanged. A successful life with ADHD is a dynamic and ever changing process.

There is NO shame in assessing your situation, identifying the need for help and then taking steps to help yourself.

Situational stress and anxiety can cause people to regress and struggle to fight the demons that exist with mental health conditions, including ADHD. We all go through times that may catapult us to a place that we need help to get balance again. Get the help you need to keep your head above the water, see through the fog, and continue on *your* victorious journey.

"When the storm rips you to pieces, you get to decide how to put yourself back together again."

— HEATHER SWINT

17

Facts About ADHD

Centers for Disease Control & Prevention Overview of ADHD: "The DSM-5TM defines ADHD as a persistent pattern of inattention and/or hyperactivity-impulsivity that interferes with functioning or development, has symptoms presenting in two or more settings (e.g. at home, school, or work; with friends or relatives; in other activities), and negatively impacts directly on social, academic or occupational functioning. Several symptoms must have been present before age 12 years." *(American Psychiatric Association. Diagnostic and Statistical Manual of Mental Disorders. Fifth edition. Washington, DC: American Psychiatric Association, 2013.)*

Individuals with ADHD may present with both inattention and hyperactivity/impulsivity, or one symptom pattern may predominate. Three presentations of ADHD are commonly referred to:

combined-type, inattentive-type and hyperactive/
impulsive-type. According to the DSM-5™
classification system, the appropriate presentation
of ADHD should be indicated based on the
predominant symptom pattern for the last
six months.

Presentations of ADHD¹

Combined

All three core features are present and ADHD is diagnosed
when ≥6 symptoms of hyperactivity/impulsivity and
≥6 symptoms of inattention have been observed for
≥6 months

Inattentive

Diagnosed if ≥6 symptoms of inattention (but <6
symptoms of hyperactivity/impulsivity) have persisted for
≥6 months

Hyperactive/Impulsive

Diagnosed if ≥6 symptoms of hyperactivity/impulsivity
(but <6 symptoms of inattention) have been present for
≥6 months

Furthermore, the DSM-5™ also states that it must be specified whether the individual with ADHD is in "partial remission" (when partial ADHD criteria have been met for the past six months with full criteria met previously, and the symptoms still result in impairment in social, academic or occupational functioning); and the current severity of the disease *(see table, page 163)*.

Current Severity of ADHD[1]

Mild

Few, if any, symptoms in excess of those required to make the diagnosis are present, and symptoms result in no more than minor impairments in social or occupational functioning

Moderate

Symptoms or functional impairment between "mild" and "severe" are present

Severe

Many symptoms in excess of those required to make the diagnosis, or several symptoms that are particularly severe, are present; or the symptoms result in marked impairment in social or occupational functioning

The term ADHD has gained popularity among the general public, in the media, and is even commonly used among professionals. Whether we call it ADD or ADHD, many are all referring to the same thing. The National Resource Center on ADHD notes "Many of the symptoms classified as ADHD symptoms of inattention are actually symptoms of executive function impairments."

Executive function refers to a wide range of central control processes in the brain that activate, integrate, and manage other brain functions.

Thomas E. Brown, Ph.D. at Yale University, compares executive function to the conductor of an orchestra. In this analogy, the conductor organizes, activates, focuses, integrates, and directs the musicians as they play, enabling the orchestra to produce complex music. Similarly, the brain's executive functions organize, activate, focus, integrate and direct, allowing the brain to perform both routine and creative work.

✔ A persistent pattern of inattention and/or hyperactivity-impulsivity that interferes with functioning or development: Six or more of the symptoms have persisted for at least six months to a degree that is inconsistent with developmental

Inattention

✔ Fails to give close attention to detail and makes careless mistakes

✔ Often does not listen when spoken to directly

✔ Has difficulty following instructions and fails to complete tasks

✔ Avoids activites that demand sustained mental effort

✔ Often loses things necessary for daily activities

✔ Often distracted by extraneous stimuli

✔ Has difficulty sustaining attention during activities and is easily distracted

✔ Has difficulty organizing tasks and activities

✔ Forgetful in daily activities

Hyperactivity

✔ Often fidgets with hands or feet or squirms in seat

✔ Often runs about or climbs excessively in situations in which it is inappropriate (in adolescents and adults, may be limited to feelings of restlessness)

✔ Often has difficulty playing or engaging in leisure activities quietly

✔ Often talks excessively

✔ Often leaves seat in classroom or in other situations in which remaining seated is expected

✔ Often is "on the go" or acts as if "driven by a motor"

Impulsivity

✔ Often interrupts or intrudes on others

✔ Often has difficulty awaiting turn

✔ Often blurts out answers before questions have been completed level and that negatively impacts directly on social and academic/occupational activities. ***Please note:*** The symptoms are not solely a manifestation of oppositional behavior, defiance, hostility, or failure to understand tasks or instructions. For older adolescents and adults (age 17 and older), five or more symptoms are required.

✔ Several inattentive or hyperactive-impulsive symptoms were present prior to age 12 years

✔ Several inattentive or hyperactive-impulsive symptoms are present in two or more settings (e.g. at home, school, or work; with friends or relatives; in other activities)

✔ There is clear evidence that the symptoms interfere with, or reduce the quality of, social, academic or occupational functioning

Three key features define attention-deficit hyperactivity disorder (ADHD)[1] or hyperkinetic disorder (HKD)[2] — inattention, hyperactivity and impulsivity — and the contribution of each to an individual's presentation of ADHD varies from patient to patient.[1] In some individuals, two or more features may contribute in equal measure; in others, one feature may predominate.[1]

As different features of ADHD can impair functioning and quality of life in different ways, it is important to accurately evaluate each patient's unique symptomatic characteristics, using medical classification systems such as the Diagnostic and Statistical Manual of Mental Disorders 5th edition (DSM-5™), or the International Classification of Mental and Behavioral Disorders 10th revision (ICD-10).[1,2] Whereas the ICD-10 characterizes HKD by its "cardinal features" of impaired inattention and overactivity, the DSM-5™ categorizes patients with ADHD by three main presentations: combined-type, predominantly inattentive-type and predominantly hyperactive-impulsive-type.

Inattention is characterized as an individual moving between tasks without completing any one activity, seemingly losing interest in one task because they become diverted to another.[1,2] Individuals with inattention are often easily distracted and forgetful, and experience difficulties when organizing activities. At school, children with ADHD may struggle to listen and be frequently distracted; in the workplace, adults with ADHD may appear as if their mind is elsewhere and their work may be messy and performed poorly.

Hyperactivity refers to excessive motor activity,[1,2] and may present differently depending on the patient's age.[1] In children, it may present as the child running and jumping around at inappropriate times, getting up from a seat when he or she is supposed to remain seated, fidgeting and wriggling, or excessive talkativeness and noisiness.[1,2] In adolescents and adults, hyperactivity may manifest as inner feelings of extreme restlessness and wearing others out with their activity *(see figure, page 163).*[1]

Impulsivity can be reckless behavior and appear impatient, and are often disinhibited in social situations. They may find it difficult to wait their turn, intruding on or interrupting others' activities or blurting out answers to a question before it has been completed.

[1,2] http://www.cdc.gov/ncbddd/adhd/data.html

http://www.adhd-institute.com/assessment-diagnosis/diagnosis/dsm-5tm/

http://www.adhd-institute.com/assessment-diagnosis/diagnosis/icd-10/

"I never lose.
I either
win or learn."

— NELSON MANDELA

18

Statistics

The Centers for Disease Control and Prevention
published the following data and statistics in 2011
regarding ADHD in the United States[1]:

The Centers for Disease Control and Prevention reports that
11% of school-age children 4 – 17 years of age (6.4 million)
have been diagnosed with ADHD as of 2011. The average
age of ADHD diagnosis was 7 years of age, but children
were reported by their parents as having more severe ADHD
were diagnosed earlier.

The percentage of children with parent-reported ADHD
diagnosis increased by 22% between the years of
2003 – 2007.

Rates of ADHD diagnosis increased an average of 3% per
year from 1997 to 2006 and an average of 5% per year from
2003 to 2011.

Boys (13.2%) were more likely than girls (5.6%) to have been
diagnosed with ADHD.

The highest rates of parent-reported ADHD diagnosis were found to be children covered by Medicaid and multiracial children.

Prevalence of parent-reported ADHD diagnosis varies by state, from a low of 5.6% in Nevada to a high of 18.7% in Kentucky.

✔ Medication Treatment:

The prevalence of children age 4 – 17 years of age taking ADHD medication increased from 4.8% in 2007 to 6.1% in 2011.

About half of preschoolers with ADHD were taking medication for ADHD and about 1 in 4 were treated with only medication.

Less than 1 in 3 children with ADHD received both medication treatment and behavioral therapy, the preferred treatment approach for children age 6 and older.

More U.S children were receiving ADHD treatment in 2011 compared to 2007; however, as many as 17.5% of children with current ADHD were not receiving medication or mental health counseling in 2011.

✔ Learning Disabilities and ADHD:

Diagnosed Attention Deficit Hyperactivity Disorder and Learning Disability: United States, 2004 – 2006 About 5% of children had ADHD without Learning Disability (LD), 5% had LD without ADHD, and 4% had both conditions.

Children 12 – 17 years of age were more likely than children 6 – 11 years of age to have each of the diagnoses.

Hispanic children were less likely than non-Hispanic white and non-Hispanic black children to have ADHD (with and without LD).

Children with Medicaid were more likely than uninsured children or privately insured children to have each of the diagnoses.

Children with each of the diagnoses were more likely than children with neither ADHD nor LD to have other chronic health conditions.

Children with ADHD (with and without LD) were more likely than children without ADHD to have contact with a mental health professional, use prescription medication, and have frequent health care visits.

✔ Peer Relationships:

Parents of children with a history of ADHD report almost 3 times as many peer problems as those without ADHD (21.1% vs. 7.3%).

Parents report that children with a history of ADHD are almost 10 times as likely to have difficulties that interfere with friendships (20.6% vs. 2.0%).

✔ Injury:

A higher percentage of parents of children with attention-deficit/hyperactivity disorder reported non-fatal injuries (4.5% vs. 2.5% for healthy children).

Children with ADHD, compared to children without ADHD, were more likely to have major injuries (59% vs. 49%), hospital inpatient (26% vs. 18%), hospital outpatient (41% vs. 33%), or emergency department admission (81% vs. 74%).

Data from international samples suggest that young people with high levels of attention difficulties are at greater risk of involvement in a motor vehicle crash, drinking and driving, and traffic violations.

✔ Economic Cost:

Using a prevalence rate of 5%, the annual societal "cost of illness" for ADHD is estimated to be between $36 and $52 billion, in 2005 dollars.

It is estimated to be between $12,005 and $17,458 annually per individual. There were an estimated 7 million ambulatory care visits for ADHD in 2006.

The total excess cost of ADHD in the US in 2000 was $31.6 billion. Of this total, $1.6 billion was for the treatment of patients, $12.1 billion was for all other health care costs of persons with ADHD, $14.2 billion was for all other health care costs of family members with ADHD, and $3.7 billion was for the work loss cost of adults with ADHD and adult family members of persons with ADHD.

ADHD creates a significant financial burden regarding the cost of medical care and work loss for patients and family members. The annual average direct cost for each per ADHD patient was $1,574, compared to $541 among matched controls.

The annual average payment (direct plus indirect cost) per family member was $2,728 for non-ADHD family members of ADHD patients versus $1,440 for family members of matched controls.

Across 10 countries, it was projected that ADHD was associated with 143.8 million lost days of productivity each year. Most of this loss can be attributed to ADHD and not co-occurring conditions.

Workers with ADHD were more likely to have at least one sick day in the past month compared to workers without ADHD.

---

[1] http://www.cdc.gov/ncbddd/adhd/data.

"We are all faced with a series of great opportunities brilliantly disguised as impossible situations."

— CHUCK SWINDOLL

Appendix

Valparaiso University College of Nursing Graduation
Picture 1995 — YAY!!

Dr. Burris' letter to graduate school admission office

Child Neurology Associates, Inc.

226 South Woods Mill Road
Suite 42 West
Chesterfield, Missouri 63017
314-275-7070
Fax 314-275-2666

James R. Rohrbaugh, M.D.
Garrett C. Burris, M.D.
David J. Callahan, M.D.

Valann Tasch, M.S.N., R.N., C.P.N.P.
Electroencephalography

December 2, 1997

RE: Kristin Kovacs   DOB: 03/30/73

To Whom It May Concern:

I'm writing to indicate that I have followed Kristin Kovacs since 1991.

In my opinion, she has documented attention deficit hyperactivity disorder. Furthermore, this was a problem that for quite a number of years in high school, as well as her early course in college, clearly interfered with her ability to perform up to her potential. She has been under my medical care and has been taking medication for treatment of attention deficit disorder. In my opinion, this medication has made a remarkable difference in her ability to focus and to think through things carefully, and in turn it has had a very significant impact, and in fact dramatic impact, on her academic performance. She is much more efficient at completing things, much more efficient at studying and recalling information, and her academic achievement and performance have clearly improved as a result.

Sincerely yours,

Garrett C. Burris, M.D.
GCB\sw t:12-12-97

cc: Kristin Kovacs
        9815 Parkway Drive
        Highland, IN 46322

Card sent from my mom when I passed CNS boards 1999 — one of the many cards of encouragement sent by my parents.

Dear Kristin,

I am so proud of you! There are so many reasons for my pride, and one is the way you set your goals and go after them. Just taking this exam is an accomplishment. You set out to take it, you prepared for it and you had the guts and determination to sit and complete it.

Great job! I am happy for all the good things in your life. Jim is a wonderful husband

as well as a great "cheer leader" for you. You have a lot of people who truly love you for who you are. All the letters behind your name are accomplishments that are nice, but it's your heart and soul that everyone loves. I am so proud of the passion you have for your job, your house, your family, and friends. That is worth everything!

I love you,

Mom

High School: Villa Duchesne, St. Louis, MO

Purdue University Transcript

Course Number	Title	Comments	Cr. Hrs. Grade Pts.
****
*	ALL INDEXES ON THIS RECORD ARE		*
*	COMPUTED ON SCALE A=4.0, F=0.0		*
****

```
1996-1997 2ND SEMESTER        0   GR O90    CALUMET
NUR  504  HOLISTIC HEALTH PROMOT           3.0 A  12.0
         CUM 4.00    3.0    12.0  SEM 4.00  3.0     12.0

1997-1998 1ST SEMESTER        0   GR O90    CALUMET
NUR -510  NURSING RESEARCH                  3.0 W
          WITHDREW 09/18/97    C
         CUM 4.00    3.0    12.0  SEM

1997-1998 2ND SEMESTER        0   GR O90    CALUMET
NUR  500  THEORET CONSTRUCTS NUR            3.0 A  12.0
NUR  506  PATHOPHYSIOLOGY                   3.0 B   9.0
         CUM 3.67    9.0    33.0  SEM 3.50  6.0     21.0

1998 SUMMER SESSION           M   GR O90    CALUMET
NUR  510  NURSING RESEARCH                  3.0 A  12.0
         CUM 3.75   12.0    45.0  SEM 4.00  3.0     12.0
```

Course Number	Title	Comments	Cr. Hrs. Grade Pts.

```
* 1998-1999 1ST SEMESTER        M   GR O90    CALUMET
* NUR  527  ETHICS FOR PROFESS NSG            3.0 A  12.0
* NUR  530  CRIT CARE NUR I                   3.0 A  12.0
* NUR  535  CRIT CARE NUR PRACT I             3.0 A  12.0
         CUM 3.86   21.0    81.0  SEM 4.00  9.0     36.0

  1998-1999 2ND SEMESTER        M   GR O90    CALUMET
EDCI 570  DEL SYS FOR ED & TRNG             3.0 A  12.0
NUR  630  CRIT CARE NUR II                  3.0 A  12.0
NUR  635  CRIT CARE NUR PRACT II            3.0 A  12.0
NUR  655  SEM PROF NURS PRACTICE            1.0 A   4.0
NUR  664  PRINS CLIN LEADERSHIP             2.0 A   8.0
         CUM 3.91   33.0   129.0  SEM 4.00 12.0     48.0

  1999 SUMMER 05/17-08/06       B   GR O90    CALUMET
NUR  599A CARDIAC PATNT LRNG NDS            3.0 A  12.0
         CUM 3.92   36.0   141.0  SEM 4.00  3.0     12.0

         MASTER OF SCIENCE
         FIELD OF STUDY: NURSING
         AWARDED FOR STUDY AT CALUMET CAMPUS
         AUGUST 6, 1999

04/99 MASTER PLAN

* * * * * * * * * END OF RECORD * * * * * * * * * *
```

Valparaiso Transcript

Course	Title	Hours	Grd	Prev	Q.P.
1991-92 TRANSF ENDING					
Univ Kansas					
CHEM 125	COLL CHEMISTRY	5.00	TR		.00
COMS 130	SPEAKR-AUD COMM	3.00	TR		.00
ENG 101	COMPOSITION	3.00	TR		.00
ENG 120	COMPOSITION&LIT	3.00	TR		.00
HPER 108	BS SKL IN:AEROB	1.00	TR		.00
PSYC 104	GEN PSYCHOLOGY	3.00	TR		.00

	Attmpt	Earned	Graded	Q.P.	GPA
Trn	18.00	18.00	.00	.00	0.000
Cum	18.00	18.00	.00	.00	0.000

Course	Title	Hours	Grd	Prev	Q.P.
1992-93 SUM I (MINI) SEM					
BIO 151	HUMAN BIOLOGY I	4.00	B-		10.80

	Attmpt	Earned	Graded	Q.P.	GPA
Sem	4.00	4.00	4.00	10.80	2.700
Cum	22.00	22.00	4.00	10.80	2.700
Nursing					

Course	Title	Hours	Grd	Prev	Q.P.
1992-93 TRANSF ENDING					
St Louis Cmty Coll Meramec-MO					
BIO 111	INTRO BIOLOGY 1	4.00	TR		.00
COM 104	PERSUASION	3.00	TR		.00
HST 101	AMER HIST 1	3.00	TR		.00
MCM 101	INTRO MASS COMM	3.00	TR		.00
MTH 160	COLLEGE ALGEBRA	4.00	TR		.00
PSC 101	INT AMER POLTCS	3.00	TR		.00
PSY 203	CHILD PSYCHOLGY	3.00	TR		.00
SOC 101	INTRO TO SOC	3.00	TR		.00

	Attmpt	Earned	Graded	Q.P.	GPA
Trn	26.00	26.00	.00	.00	0.000
Cum	48.00	48.00	4.00	10.80	2.700

Course	Title	Hours	Grd	Prev	Q.P.
1993-94 SUMMER II SEM					
HIST 100	HIS W THOT&SOC	3.00	B		9.00

	Attmpt	Earned	Graded	Q.P.	GPA
Sem	3.00	3.00	3.00	9.00	3.000
Cum	51.00	51.00	7.00	19.80	2.828

Course	Title	Hours	Grd	Prev	Q.P.
1993-94 FALL SEM					
BIO 210	MICROBIOLOGY	4.00	B-		10.80
NUR 205	PROF ROLE/NURSG	3.00	B+		9.90
NUR 206	PHYSICAL ASSESS	2.00	B-		5.40
SOC 150	INTRO TO ANTHRO	3.00	B		9.00

Course	Title	Hours	Grd	Prev	Q.P.
THEO 100	INTR CHRST THEO	3.00	A		12.00

	Attmpt	Earned	Graded	Q.P.	GPA
Sem	15.00	15.00	15.00	47.10	3.140
Cum	66.00	66.00	22.00	66.90	3.040
Nursing					

Course	Title	Hours	Grd	Prev	Q.P.
1993-94 SPRING SEM					
HE 260	HUMAN NUTRITION	3.00	B+		9.90
NUR 215	CLIN APPLICATN OF PROFL ROLE	4.00	C+		9.20
NUR 220	PRIM CARE FAM	3.00	B-		8.10
NUR 310	US HLTH CARE SYSTEMS	3.00	W		.00
NUR 315	INTR NURSG RSCH	3.00	C+		6.90

	Attmpt	Earned	Graded	Q.P.	GPA
Sem	13.00	13.00	13.00	34.10	2.623
Cum	79.00	79.00	35.00	101.00	2.885
Nursing					

Course	Title	Hours	Grd	Prev	Q.P.
1993-94 SUM I (MINI) SEM					
NUR 340	SEC CARE PSYCH	4.00	B-		10.80

	Attmpt	Earned	Graded	Q.P.	GPA
Sem	4.00	4.00	4.00	10.80	2.700
Cum	83.00	83.00	39.00	111.80	2.866

Course	Title	Hours	Grd	Prev	Q.P.
1994-95 SUMMER II SEM					
NUR 330	SEC CARE ADULT &LONG LVD ADULT	4.00	R	C-	.00

	Attmpt	Earned	Graded	Q.P.	GPA
Sem	4.00	.00	.00	.00	0.000
Cum	87.00	83.00	39.00	111.80	2.866

Course	Title	Hours	Grd	Prev	Q.P.
1994-95 FALL SEM					
NUR 310	US HLTH CARE SYSTEMS	3.00	B		9.00
NUR 320	SEC CARE PARENT	5.00	B		15.00
NUR 330	SEC CARE ADULT &LONG LVD ADULT	4.00	C		8.00
THEO 230	THE CHRSTN FAIT	3.00	A-		11.10

	Attmpt	Earned	Graded	Q.P.	GPA
Sem	15.00	15.00	15.00	43.10	2.873
Cum	102.00	98.00	54.00	154.90	2.868
Nursing					

Course	Title	Hours	Grd	Prev	Q.P.
1994-95 SPRING SEM					
NUR 420	TERT CARE ISS	3.00	B-		8.10
NUR 430	SEC CARE ADULT& LONG LVD AD II	4.00	B-		10.80
NUR 435	TERT CARE ADLT LONG-LVD ADULT	4.00	B-		10.80
NUR 440	TERT CARE/PSYCH NURSING	2.00	B-		5.40
THEO 324	AMER REL EXPER	3.00	A		12.00

	Attmpt	Earned	Graded	Q.P.	GPA
Sem	16.00	16.00	16.00	47.10	2.943
Cum	118.00	114.00	70.00	202.00	2.885
Nursing					

Course	Title	Hours	Grd	Prev	Q.P.
1994-95 SUM I (MINI) SEM					
NUR 410	TERT CARE COMM	5.00	B		15.00
NUR 450	NURSG MGMT IN HLTH CARE SYSTM	4.00	C+		9.20

	Attmpt	Earned	Graded	Q.P.	GPA
Sem	9.00	9.00	9.00	24.20	2.688
Cum	127.00	123.00	79.00	226.20	2.863

Course	Title	Hours	Grd	Prev	Q.P.
1995-96 SUMMER II SEM					
NUR 480	PROF ROLE PRAC	4.00	S		.00
PSY 201	STATISTICL METH	3.00	C		6.00

	Attmpt	Earned	Graded	Q.P.	GPA
Sem	7.00	7.00	3.00	6.00	2.000
Cum	134.00	130.00	82.00	232.20	2.831

** END OF RECORD **

179

Email from Dr. Janet Brown, Dean of the College of Nursing at Valparaiso University

From: Janet Brown
To: Mary Kovacs
Date: Monday - April 28, 2008 5:47 PM
Subject: Re: Thank You

Kristin,

Not a day has gone by that I haven't thought of you. Karen gave me the news and expressed that you really wanted to deliver the news in person. I apologize for being so booked up. I would have liked to visit with you and express to you directly how much I appreciate all that you contributed this past semester. You are an excellent instructor. You have high professional standards, follow through with what you start, and are a real role model for students. All that had you can't say enough about you and how you have influenced them personally and professionally. I had big ideas for you here at Valpo so I was very sorry to hear that you are relocating. But I am thrilled for you and your family in that you can return to family and, of course, for your husband as he is obviously valued in his position.

Best wishes to you as you relocate. I hope you will find ways to be involved in nursing in some capacity. You are too valuable a resource to sit on the shelf for too long.
Dean Brown

"When I stand before
God at the end of my life,
I hope that I put to work
every bit of passion
and love and can say,
'I used the gifts You gave
me. Thank you for the
opportunity to live
a full and happy life'. "

— Kristin Seymour

about the author...

Kristin Seymour is a board certified Adult Health Clinical Nurse Specialist with ADHD.

Kristin consults with parents of children with ADHD, principals, and peers to discuss diagnostic processes and factors needed for success.

Kristin works as a Clinical Nurse Specialist at the Washington University Heart & Vascular Center at Barnes-Jewish Hospital in St. Louis, Missouri. She is an active member at the state level on the Missouri Time Critical Diagnosis (TCD) task force. Her involvement with TCD legislation is related to the education of clinical staff, as well as implementation of the legislation statewide.

Kristin is a member of the American College of Cardiology and is considered an expert on cardiac conditions such as Congestive Heart Failure and Sudden Cardiac Arrest. Kristin has been a clinical cardiology expert with Johnson & Johnson speaker's bureau since 2003.

Kristin lives in St. Louis with her husband of 19 years, Jim, and their two daughters.

notes

Made in the USA
Middletown, DE
04 June 2018